Praise for *B State*

"He's done it again! Mark Samuel has written another compelling, relevant, and engaging book on how to move an organization from 'A State' to 'B State.' Beyond organizational accountability, Samuel's practical tips and critical insight help leaders effectively drive organizational performance to meet desired outcomes and goals. Very seldom today do you read business books that deliver an 'aha' moment. *B State* does not disappoint; it is a must-read for any executive."

—Jim Barnes, CEO of enVista

"Reading Mark's real stories of people and organizations stuck in the 'A State' will cause most readers to shudder from personal recognition. But his journey of self-reflection and revelation results in a unique process for escaping this state. Through the clear illustration and results of his transformational process to the 'B State,' we begin to see how to exit our victim status and create our own picture of success. Mark generously shares his learnings and discoveries in *B State*, empowering everyone who reads it to know how to become 'unstuck.'"

—Sue Bingham, Founder of HPWP (High Performance Work Place)
and co-author of *Creating the High Performance Work Place*

"If you're tired of the same repetitive loops, personally or professionally, it's time to come up for a breath of fresh air with Mark Samuel's *B State*. Mark reveals a truly breakthrough way of leaving behind the endless loops of frustration that I call Conscious Business. Break on through to the other side!"

—Russell Bishop, author of *Workarounds That Work* and
CEO of Conscious Living

"*B State* shows leaders and managers the power of breaking out of silos to communicate and collaborate in a new way, leading to the sustainable results organizations are starving for. Mark Samuel proposes a simple, revolutionary mind-set shift and an approach that is life-changing for all leaders, managers, and the companies they work for on all levels, professionally and personally."

—Rúna Bouius, transformational leadership expert, speaker, and author

"Mark's book and work—especially his focus on Collective Execution—resonate strongly with me. The concept of collectively achieving and executing on goals is reflective of the goals of Best Practice Institute programs; you get the best and most rapid results out of your programs not by over-analyzing your current state but by focusing on your future state and what needs to be done."

—Louis Carter, CEO of Best Practice Institute and coauthor of *The Change Champion's Field Guide* and *Best Practices in Talent Management*

"Mark is a visionary and an original thinker. He can walk into any dysfunctional situation and diagnose the root cause of it. He sees the best possible outcome and knows how to get you there faster than you expected. This book teaches you how to do that for yourself, your team, and your company."

—Sophie Chiche, Founder and CEO of Shape House

"I have focused on business and organizational transformation for the last 25 years, and I can attest that the key levers that Mark describes in this book actually do work: a powerful shared purpose, collaborative vs. siloed priorities, a forward focus on building positive energy, and scale vs. dwelling on the problem—these are the pillars of a successful transformation."

—Victor Cho, CEO of Evite™

"Mark Samuel has created a new paradigm in thinking about how to address the major challenges facing business today. He provides a step-by-step roadmap for companies to move from an 'A State' culture to a 'B State' culture, showing them how to achieve the kind of inclusive environment that has engaged employees and leaders and loyal consumers. *B State* is a must-read for business leaders and anyone who wants to build a world class organization."

—Al Cornish, System Vice President of Learning & Organizational Development and Chief Learning Officer at Norton Healthcare

"Mark Samuel's *B State* takes accountability to higher breakthrough levels and is a must-read for all leaders at any level of the organization. While the subject is complicated, Mark makes it simple and easy to read and follow. His use of real life stories, personal and professional, truly delivers the message of breakthrough performance. It provides a practical roadmap to creating the future rather than trying to predict it, a future with outstanding results and high-performing culture. I was energized and inspired by the many golden nuggets of learnings in this book, and I plan on using them in both my personal and professional development."
—Fadi Diya, Senior Vice President and Chief Nuclear Officer at Amaren, Corp.

"Mark Samuel is a proven expert on leadership and breakthrough results. His knowledge of the workplace, its challenges, and the tools to overcome those challenges, leads to a powerful and significant read for all business owners, managers, and supervisors. His roadmap for success, *B State*, helps teams break down silo behavior, produces excellent teamwork throughout the organization, and truly drives outcomes and results. Without Mark Samuel's guidance using the *B State* concepts, our road to becoming a Legacy Organization would not be nearly as clear as it is. Thank you, Mark, for writing such a valuable and influential book."

—Frank Dulcich, CEO and President of Pacific Seafood Group

"Looking for a way to build self-awareness in an impactful way? This book provides abundant practical and savvy advice, for leaders and individual contributors alike, on how to move with confidence toward desired outcomes. It's a home run!"
—Gene Gerrard, Vice President of Human Resources, TOTE

"Mark Samuel provides a highly useful roadmap to a higher level of functioning he calls 'B State.' Business leaders everywhere could benefit from reading this book and applying its powerful tools. I urge you to make it a priority to read this book and get to work creating B State in your own life and work."
—Gay Hendricks, PhD, president of The Hendricks Institute
and author of *The Big Leap*

"Mark Samuel's *B State* is a paradigm shift to quickly transform your business and culture by changing your "habits of collective execution." This is not only a refreshing approach that gets measurable results but also a must-read for executives and leaders."

—Joey Hubbard, Global Head of Trainings at Thrive Global

"*B State* is a roadmap to transformational change, dealing with all aspects of accountability and change. The 'Middle Management Miracle' alone can create lasting change—quickly—in an organization."

—Mark Jesty, Chairman, Institute for Management Studies, Canada

"Mark Samuel's model for achieving 'B State' is built on methodically shaping an organization's leadership culture to support the desired state. Using Mark's B State process, our leadership team transformed its habits of execution, nurtured new levels of accountability within mid-management, and significantly exceeded our performance goals."

—Susan V. Juris, President of University Hospitals Ahuja Medical Center

"The B State methodology presented in Mark's book is fast and transformational. Our worldwide marketing company with over 150 employees and contractors streamlined our systems, improved our productivity, and provided our customers with even greater responsiveness. And, many remarked about the positive impact in their own personal lives."

—Sinan Kanatsiz, CEO of KCOMM

"*B State* describes in detail the approach used by Mark to transform my leadership team and company. It's practical, fast, and got us through a difficult transition with alignment and cooperation in which everyone felt safe."

—Praful Kulkarni, PhD, CEO of gkkworks, Principal & Director of Integrated Services for CannonDesign

"*B State* resonates strongly with me because it's a practical approach to transformation. Using the techniques outlined in his book, Mark helped our organization focus on the Collective Execution and the future state of what needed to be done—the 'B State.' We have transformed to a new B State, and it is like being a new organization. This is a model that works and a book that can transform your organization and/or your personal life very quickly."

—Ron Peterson, President and CEO of Baxter Regional Medical Center

"Mark uses authentic and tangible examples—like stories about drumming, baseball, and how these relate to business—to bring important business concepts to life for me. As he points out, why do we have so many dysfunctions in business if it is so clear in music and sports that there's a better way? How we work together, our attitudes, behaviors, and actions are the key to our transformation. The concepts in *B State* are timely and applicable to the multiple generations in the workforce. I believe they can bring people together to change the world."

—Darwin Richardson, Senior Vice President of Quality
and Regulatory Affairs at BPL Plasma

"Mark has brought us a powerful concept and methodology for getting unstuck and moving to a new future. This system is more keenly focused on the future we want rather than the navel gazing most companies utilize in their change management processes. From my experience, his thinking goes deeper into shaping that future, complete with our attitudes, motivations, clarity of behaviors, and new desired states. Then he adds the lasting ingredient of accountability. Mark always gets me to think on the next level, and this book has loads to support that assessment."

—Craig Robbins, Coach, Advisor Development,
and formerly Chief Knowledge Officer of Colliers International

"I applaud and am thankful for Mark's wisdom and insights on transforming organizations, bringing them to higher levels of awareness and success. *B State* clearly shows how positive, honest, and reflective practices can bring out the best in individuals, families, businesses, and our society. Mark Samuel has laid the framework for bridging learning and leading with courageous loving!"

—Stu Semigran, Cofounder and President of EduCare Foundation, Los Angeles' largest after school program provider

"Mark Samuel is a proven expert on accountability. He wisely recognizes that every great leader must set the right team and also be very decisive to be successful. Apply the wisdom of *B State*, and you'll see the transforming effect on your team. If you really want to achieve great results in your organization and to be able to do it fast, this book will help you take the necessary steps to get there."

—Juan José Valdés Torres, CEO of Adama México

"*B State* energized me, and I clearly see the potential of applying all these steps to my organization. Mark Samuel captured the path to breakthrough transformation through this book and its message."

—Michael van Praag, President of the Royal Dutch Soccer Association

"Mark Samuel's *B State* allows organizations to create a compelling picture of the future. His book is the true source of clarity on what leadership needs to focus on: the most critical and the most cross-functional. Most accountability experts forget about the cross-functional side—the key to Marks' model. *B State* blends future focus into measurable outcomes and habits of execution that create the playbook for transforming leadership and results in your organization."

—Elaine Vincent, Chief Administrative Officer, Town of Okotoks

"When you go to the gym and are lifting weights properly, you feel sore afterward and see transformation of the muscle. Welcome to the journey to B State as Mark Samuel takes your teams on a leadership transformation that produces rapid and measurable results!"

—Abbas Yar-Khan, Vice President of Manufacturing, Shire

B STATE

A NEW ROADMAP *for*
BOLD LEADERSHIP, **BRAVE** CULTURE,
and **BREAKTHROUGH** RESULTS

B STATE

MARK SAMUEL

GREENLEAF
BOOK GROUP PRESS

Published by Greenleaf Book Group Press
Austin, Texas
www.gbgpress.com

Distributed by Greenleaf Book Group

For ordering information or special discounts for bulk purchases, please contact Greenleaf Book Group at PO Box 91869, Austin, TX 78709, 512.891.6100.

Design and composition by Greenleaf Book Group
Cover design by Greenleaf Book Group
Cover images: ©iStockphoto.com/alashi and ©iStockphoto.com/yogysic

Publisher's Cataloging-in-Publication data is available.

Print ISBN: 978-1-62634-569-0

eBook ISBN: 978-1-62634-570-6

Part of the Tree Neutral® program, which offsets the number of trees consumed in the production and printing of this book by taking proactive steps, such as planting trees in direct proportion to the number of trees used: www.treeneutral.com

TreeNeutral

Printed in the United States of America on acid-free paper

18 19 20 21 22 23   10 9 8 7 6 5 4 3 2 1

First Edition

To our community of clients, consultants, and associates who have courageously cocreated B State— a new paradigm for leading organizations, communities, and families with greater purpose, psychological safety, accountability, and breakthrough results.

A special appreciation goes to all B State clients who have openly shared their challenges and successes with authenticity, vulnerability, and commitment. This book couldn't have been written without you.

Contents

Foreword

You could call Mark Samuel something of a magician. He's an innovative, pioneering management consultant who—I'm not kidding—seems to work magic in organizations. With his skillful touch, stalled companies fire back up into productivity; companies that were stuck shake loose and find their freedom and flow.

It's kind of like magic.

We've been in awe of his amazing results and hoped to someday work with him to help us sort out our own team's challenges. But there's only one of him, and there are countless others who could use his insights. We'd have to get in line.

But the good news here is the generous gift of this book that Mark Samuel has written, which gives us a way to understand and maybe even adopt the new mind-set, strategies, systems, and tools that produce his magic. Mark shares and explains in a passionately personal way (even applying his ideas to family meetings and marriage) the principles and methods behind the startling results that his consulting work produces.

For anyone interested in transforming a sluggish organization, this is a book of revelations.

To begin with, Mark shines an unsparing, harsh spotlight on organizations that are stuck in their dysfunctional ways. He calls out the favoritism, cowardice, and low levels of accountability and consciousness that pervade so many organizations that are trapped inside what he calls an "A State" culture. This is a hopeless culture that has previously seemed almost inherent in organizations. A fact of life. It is what it is.

But here, we see it as surprisingly optional because this "A State" is not built in. In fact, it is perpetuated by the behaviors and attitudes of those trying to manage. In Mark's words, these inefficient behaviors and demoralizing attitudes "cannot be resolved by core values, strategic plans, additional metrics, process improvements, or training programs, because they are *accepted team habits*, even though they foster perpetual frustration, inefficiency, wasted resources, and burnout."

Where was this book when I needed it? What would have happened to the public relations company I owned and ran all those years ago that finally went bankrupt? What if we'd had this book? I could see, as I read this book for the second time, that the bankruptcy would not have occurred because I would have been enlightened as to what Mark calls the "B State," a fearless state of innovation, evolution, and internal collaboration.

What about all the corporate training I did years after that for companies stuck in "A State" paralysis? I do think the training was good, but as Mark reveals, all the training in the world can't save an organization whose internal behaviors and attitudes remain unchanged.

Perhaps this is why so many CEOs have said to me, in morose voices, "Well . . . training comes and training goes, and nothing's ever different."

Well, not until now. Not if you read and apply the insights in this book.

The ideas behind Mark Samuel's consulting "magic" are hereby revealed. And you can apply these ideas yourself if you read this book carefully and implement what's here. The creation of a highly functional "B State" organization or team (or family) is laid out for you like never before. Those of us who've known Mark and wondered "How does he do that?" don't have to wonder anymore.

This book offers case histories to illustrate Mark's concepts, making the overall effect feel experiential—transformational versus informational. It's one thing to grasp intellectually that moving (by agreement, not decree) to a "B State" leads to having a team wherein "people with clear direction and expectations feel safe, engaged, and supported," but it's even better when the stories drop in, reach your heart, and help you get things at the deepest level.

Mark doesn't hang us up in statistical business studies about the hidden role of energy in the workplace. Instead, he tells a family story about his wife and young daughter, so rather than just seeing the logic of it, we see the *truth* of it. If you don't want to remain stuck in an "A State," understanding the flow of energy, and its contagious nature, is vital.

The legendary business analyst W. Edwards Deming said that the key to restoring health and vitality to an organization is to "drive fear out." You can understand Deming's idea in theory, but how exactly do you do that? The path has always been painfully unclear. With Mark's book, this becomes as simple and clear as going from A to B, or as Mark would say, from an "A State" to a "B State."

The solutions in this book are both simple and profound. You'll also see that Mark draws on his background in athletics and music to illustrate the importance of energy awareness in a "B State" organization.

Many companies and teams spend hours composing mission statements and slogans. Sometimes you see the words up on a conference room wall or highlighted on a website. For an "A State" company, that seems to be enough.

But not here. Not if you want to thrive and become "B State." Mark challenges leaders to go deeper than the mere slogan level and commit to "do differently," applying behaviors that will actually have the power to transform a culture and strengthen the bottom line.

Even more, the solutions that run through this book have a consistent theme of *inclusion*. When you apply the concepts, team members feel safe, supported, and *included* in your mission. The traditional "A State" old boys' culture of secrecy, hierarchy, micromanagement, and favoritism is exposed as the very source of institutional paralysis.

Fortunately for us, the "B State" presented here is full of specific and doable cures for this paralysis, this company-wide feeling of being stuck.

It's perhaps not a surprise that Mark Samuel is a former musician, a drummer. In every good band, the drummer is the one who pulls it all together. With the beat and the rhythm the drummer sets, we play together. When we're good, and the beat is strong and clear, we play as one. When that happens, the music that results is as captivating and moving as this book.

Steve Chandler
Business and life coach and founder of the Coaching Prosperity School

Birmingham, Michigan
February 2018

Introduction

Nothing is worse than feeling stuck.

Whether your organization cannot seem to move forward or you're paralyzed in your personal life, the result is the same: frustration and confusion. It's almost a feeling of hopelessness when you think about how much effort you've put in, how much money you've spent on outside expertise, how many different things you've tried—and yet, nothing has really changed.

And you think, "Maybe it never will."

I call that existing in the "A State."

In the A State, your organization cannot possibly keep up with today's urgency to beat the competition, respond to fluctuating market conditions, or satisfy ever-increasing customer expectations. No matter how much time and resources you spend on "continuous process improvement," "skill building," "leadership programs," "team-building exercises," "lean and agile systems," and "culture-shaping regimens," you cannot maintain your market share or profitability ratio. Your culture is stuck in archaic silos. Workers, supervisors, middle and senior managers, and executives resort to the "blame game" to justify breakdowns. Few issues ever get satisfactorily, much less permanently, resolved. And power struggles, bureaucracy, and old-school mind-sets prevent your younger, more tuned-in leaders from having any innovative impact.

Yup, you're stuck.

In the *individual* A State, you cannot make your relationships work, find the job or career path that makes you happy, or maintain the diet/exercise regimen you *swore* to your friends and family—and doctor—you'd keep up to feel better. No matter how many personal-growth workshops you go to, how much positive thinking you employ, how many affirmations you dutifully write out, or how many life coaches, therapists, and gurus you follow, you cannot seem to get out of your own way.

You're still discouraged—maybe even depressed. You still look for someone or something to "complete" you. You still pray for a miracle from every lottery ticket. You still cannot talk to your kids . . . or siblings . . . or parents without coming away upset. You still hope the next pill, supplement, or organic concoction will fill you up and take away the gnawing hole in your psyche. You still wonder what you're doing with your life and whether anyone will ever love you—and if they do, for how long?

Yeah, you're stuck.

Time to move into the "B State."

Join us in growing the B State Community and benefit from rich resources and the opportunity to network with your peers on a similar journey. Visit www.BState.com/bonus to get access to videos, webinars, and other tools on how to draft and refine your B State to deliver breakthrough results.

1

Stuck in "A State"

*When one door closes, another opens; but we often look
so long and so regretfully upon the closed door that
we do not see the one which has opened for us.*

—ALEXANDER GRAHAM BELL

A manufacturing company experienced too many injuries because plant employees didn't follow posted safety protocols. As in any A State organization, management's solution was to send those employees to a safety-procedure training program. That is the definition of an A State, after all: using past and current mind-sets and behaviors to try to make changes or improvements. But after putting in the time and effort to schedule the program, management discovered their plant employees had already completed the exact same program *seven times*. They'd even earned certificates of completion.

Naturally, everyone was frustrated about the waste of time and resources—and obviously, another round of training would not solve the problem.

Does this circular trap sound familiar? How many times do we send people to training programs that do not produce any meaningful behavior changes or performance improvement? We think we're doing something, when, in fact, we're simply moving from being stuck in an A State to being stuck in an "A+ State," wherein we make one or more incremental improvements toward our goals but nothing really changes. We're still bogged down—just at a slightly higher, more educated level. We still haven't addressed the real challenges blocking our success.

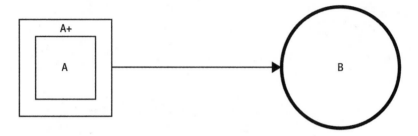

Figure 1: A to A+ Continuous Improvement

That's where transforming to a B State culture comes in. B State—short for "breakthrough" change—encompasses a new mind-set and habits of behavior that rapidly produce and sustain a *transformational* future. B State is a paradigm shift in thinking and behavior that produces a dynamic forward launch.

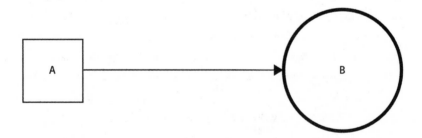

Figure 2: A State to B State Transformation

A Different Perspective

Culture is how decisions are made, challenges
are faced, and problems are handled.
When visiting any organization, the culture can be felt.

–Sue Bingham, author of
Creating the High Performance Work Place

Tom, the CIO of "Milstun Corporation," a large multinational manufacturing company based in Germany, had been given three and a half years to reduce costs and duplication of effort, streamline processes, and improve internal customer satisfaction by centralizing his two thousand–person information systems (IS) department.

Tom knew his leadership team had to assess all the systems that needed changing, develop a model to centralize the organization, and create a strategic plan to get the job done, so he brought in the most recognized, best-in-the-world consulting firms to help. For two years, the leadership team attended team-building programs, leadership-development workshops, change-management presentations, process-improvement seminars, and project-management training. After developing new skills for two years, all the leaders considered themselves a "better team."

But nothing actually changed. No real movement toward centralization could occur because the team members reneged on the commitments they made (in whatever the latest "outside" program they'd attended) just as soon as they got back to their respective divisions in Asia, the United States, and Europe.

All that training merely moved them from being stuck in A State to being stuck in an A+ State. After two years, they still equated "centralizing" with "giving up control," and no one was willing to do that—yet. But Tom knew that if they didn't centralize by the board's deadline, his entire department would be outsourced, which meant a lot of his people would lose their jobs. As outrageous as that sounds, he'd seen it happen before.

By the time he called me in, Tom felt like a failure—an exasperated, angry failure.

"It may be too late for your help," he admitted when we first met. "I've already wasted two years on too many failed change efforts. Now we only have a year and a half to completely restructure, change our technical processes across the entire organization, and create a new culture. I don't think we have enough time left. I blew it."

"No, you didn't," I assured him. "We can produce a centralized organization, complete with culture change, in eighteen months or less. We just have to create a clear 'Picture of Success,' focus on middle management instead of your senior team, and develop new 'Team Habits of Collective Execution.'"

"Wait a minute," Tom protested. "Every other consultant has said we have to change our senior management team first, not our middle managers."

"I'm sure they did," I responded. "And they've taken up two years of your time trying to do that. We've discovered that middle managers are the true change agents—*if* they operate as a unified team."

"Really? Okay, I guess that makes sense. And I have wasted so much time trying to change the senior managers without any progress. So it's great that we can put the focus on middle management to make this change."

"Oh, there is one more thing." I said. "You'll have to tell your people we only have a year to get it done—not a year and a half."

"What! I can't do that! There's no way we can make such a massive change in a year! It's physically impossible!"

"Then I won't do the project."

"Are you kidding me? Why not?"

I smiled. "Because people need a sense of urgency, or they'll put off any kind of change to the last possible moment—especially if that change is uncomfortable, disruptive, and increases their workload. That's just human nature. So we need your team's 'last possible moment' to be *right now!* Plus, there's a built-in sense of uncertainty in this kind of thing, especially since no one knows how to do this and everything else they've tried so far has failed. We need that sense of urgency to overcome all that.

"Besides," I added, "if we get off schedule, we'll still have six more months to make it work."

Tom's shoulders dropped. "Okay, okay, that makes sense. Not to mention you're my last resort. I'll tell you what—if you'll commit to not try to change my senior management team and just focus on my middle managers, then I'll commit to telling my people this needs to be accomplished in a year. I just don't want the lack of change in my senior management team to become the excuse for you like it was for other consultants."

"Agreed."

"Fine," he said. "Write up the proposal. We've got a deal."

My proposal was completely different from anything else Tom had ever experienced. It didn't include developing shared values, solving breakdowns, or implementing a traditional change-management process. Tom admitted he really didn't understand our approach, but when I started to explain, he cut me off.

"Forget it. I can't afford to keep using the same traditional approaches that haven't worked for two years," he said, clearly exasperated. "I'll take a risk on you and . . . whatever your 'B State' is."

We began our weeklong assessment by talking with various middle and a few senior managers. "I know you don't want senior management to be part of this," I told Tom when he protested, "but we need to include them to identify breakdowns and ensure appropriate linkage with middle managers. We need to find out if people really understand what it means to be centralized."

As it turned out, most of them didn't. Only Tom and Frank, the brilliant but hot-blooded subject-matter expert (SME) who had created the model they'd been trying to implement for two years, had any sense of what a centralized organization looked like.

After completing all the other interviews, we visited Frank to make sure we understood his vision and model. It seemed pretty simple to us, but we weren't technical experts in their industry—maybe we were oversimplifying his concepts. But as we explained our understanding to him, he jumped up excitedly.

"Yes! That's it! Finally! Someone gets this! I'm so frustrated and angry with all the other managers. How can they not understand it? Why do they keep trying to make it so much more complicated?"

It's human nature to make change more complicated than it needs to be, especially when we don't really want to change, even if we know we have to. That's why people don't go to doctors, leave bad positions or relationships, or move forward in their lives. They don't want to leave their comfort zone.

We gathered about sixty senior and middle managers from three continents to a single meeting in Munich. We didn't talk to them about centralizing the organization, or about creating a new leadership model, or about any of the other topics they expected. Instead, we introduced the B State concept and transformation process, and we talked about creating a clear Picture of Success for the fully operational and effective centralized IS department:

That picture will include not only your final result, but also new behaviors about cross-functional coordination, teamwork, and problem-solving that need to become new habits. Your role as leaders will naturally expand during the course of this process. It's unavoidable. You're going to move from only controlling your own area to sharing leadership and ownership so you all mutually get to where you need to go.

While some of the managers were excited to hear about our different approach, most were admittedly skeptical—but they were all willing to participate because Tom and I presented the change as nonnegotiable.

"There really is no choice here," I told them. "If you don't centralize, your department will be outsourced. It's that simple."

When those sixty people left the working session after going through our B State transformation process, they not only understood Frank's model, but had aligned their expectations with it, formed task forces to implement the "Team Habits of Collective Execution" necessary to create a B State culture, chosen the eight projects that would take priority during the change, and accepted a shared-ownership project-management process—if one of the eight project teams failed, they all failed. Plus, they created their own follow-up system to support and hold each other, and the group, accountable.

They did all that in only three days.

The major centralization shift was completed in nine months—three months sooner than the "urgent deadline" we gave them and nine months sooner than their real deadline. They completed the full transformation by month twelve—six months ahead of the CIO's schedule.

Although we never addressed performance improvement, several side benefits of transitioning to the B State surfaced. The top-prioritized technical projects came in 100 percent on time/on budget for the first time. Overall project performance rose from 25 percent on time/on budget to 75 percent. Key performance indicators (KPIs) went up 50 percent. Operating expenses decreased and internal customer satisfaction increased, producing break-through results.

Best of all, fifteen relationship factors—including trust, support, and conflict resolution—improved 35 percent throughout the entire management team.

For me, the icing on the cake came when one of the company's primary vendors stood up at the meeting where all these statistics were revealed and said, "You know what? Before we started this change effort, we considered you our worst customer. Now you're our best—thanks to the problem-solving and decision-making improvements in our partnership."

After the meeting broke up, Tom told me, "Our results have been so dramatic, Mark, they've blown everyone away. I mean, most of our managers were so skeptical when you first walked in the door, but now they understand the real meaning behind B State Collective Execution and how you can really take us to another level! They want to expand it to other areas of our department, but I was wondering about something else—especially in light of what our vendor just said."

"Okay. What do you need?"

"We operate in an us-versus-them customer-supplier environment with most of our vendors. Can you help us improve our partnerships with them?"

"Sure! But we'd have to work with them first, by themselves, to improve their own execution. In other words, we'd have to change their mind-set and habits of execution to prepare them to be better partners."

"Let's do it!" Tom said. "And we'll pay for it."

I'd believed in the B State before, but this success was so enormous it made me realize B State transformations not only worked faster than I thought they would, but could cross every kind of barrier, be it language, distance, individual resistance, time zones, or even culture.

It was a life-changing moment for me.

2

My B State Discovery Journey

*The same thinking that has led you to where you are
is not going to lead you to where you want to go.*

—ALBERT EINSTEIN

As a typical team-building facilitator back in 1983, I had just completed a program with a leadership team, using all the standard methods. We created an aligned vision statement. We did a styles survey so people could better understand each other. I had the participants do team activities and action plans to apply their "awareness" and "team experience" to their "workplace goals and challenges."

If the positive evaluations at the end of the program were to be believed, my program was a huge success.

Three months later, I visited the company to do a follow-up meeting with the team leader and ran across several team members. They were all excited to share how much they had benefited from our work together. One person even said, "It changed my life!"

I was on top of the world, my ego and self-esteem growing with every word of praise. Of course, I had to ask: "How's the leadership team doing?"

"Oh, it's still as dysfunctional as usual—everyone's still fighting about everything—but we all agree the team building was great for our individual growth!"

So much for my swelling ego! I felt like a failure as my heart sank to the floor. Sure, I was happy for everyone's wonderful personal growth, but that wasn't what I'd been hired to do. I was supposed to build the team.

And I hadn't.

"For a while," the woman continued as I barely listened, "the team was working better, and the impact was very positive. But two months later, people were back to their old behaviors.

"We're stuck again."

I don't even remember whether I met with the leader that day. I know I went home depressed. After all, I had used the methodology learned from my graduate-school mentor, a leading organization-development expert, professor, and practicing consultant. I had carefully followed in his footsteps so I could provide substantial value to my clients by building teams and helping people in a meaningful, long-lasting way.

Had I been fooling myself?

I prided myself on my high level of integrity, so I decided right then that if I couldn't figure out how to help teams last on their own in an improved state for at least one year, I'd change careers. I was tired of consultants and trainers who made promises of better effectiveness but didn't deliver lasting results, and I wasn't about to join that group and live in hypocrisy just because it paid well.

My mentor trained me better than that.

I went back and analyzed every team and organization I had ever worked with, looking for some commonality, some pattern of breakdown. And I found it—at the same point after every team-building program in every organization. Even though everyone reported feeling improved trust, support, and dedication while we worked together, their day-to-day challenges had undermined those commitments after three months back in the workplace. Follow-through soon broke down, and the trust and support they'd so eagerly built together fell apart.

It didn't take me long to realize why: none of the teams—or the team members themselves—felt answerable for their commitments or agreements, so they had no *reason* to live up to them.

It all came down to accountability—which, I discovered over the next two years, is a moving target. No matter what I did to change my team-building methodology, each solution only worked for about three months before another issue popped up. People would take responsibility for their behaviors—they stopped bickering, for example—but six months later a lack of follow-through on priority projects created another breakdown. Nine months later, another issue popped up when new hires weren't properly "on-boarded" into their team culture.

Enough was enough. Even though I'd been a "good student" all my life and followed my professors' teachings diligently, I stopped reading popular management books during those two years. I did not refer to what I'd learned from other consultants and advisors. I divorced myself from my core beliefs about change management and building teams. I even gave up my "sacred cows"—those theories I *knew for a fact* were correct because they *made perfect sense.*

> *If I'm going to truly approach this challenge as a scientist, I have to be as impartial as possible. I have to let each situation be my teacher. I have to "pray" for solutions when I have none, using an instinctive self-hypnotic meditative state to let my subconscious show me the answer.*

It was a scary, uncomfortable period in my life, probably because I still thought of myself primarily as a jock and a musician. Sure, I liked team building, but I never considered myself creative or innovative. I wasn't a "thinker" like my college roommate Chip Clitheroe, who once invited me to a retreat to "think about thinking." The only things I wanted to think about were hiking and boating. As far as I was concerned, I was just tweaking what my mentor had taught me. I set a goal for myself, a new criterion for success: to have a team function effectively on their own for a year without needing my support.

We accomplished that by the end of the second year.

Then we did it again with another team. And another one. I didn't have to change careers! I had created a repeatable, systemic approach that consistently resulted in lasting team success.

A few months later when another company asked me to submit a proposal for team building, I wrote up the methodology I'd just discovered, which had worked so well for my last client.

"Well," the manager said during our interview, "I like your proposal and approach, but it's *not* team building."

"What are you talking about?" I demanded. "Team building is the only thing I know!"

"Hey, I've got a pile of proposals here for team building, and none of them are anything like what you've written."

I left the interview shocked, my very identity challenged, and immediately sought out my mentor for a reality check. "Isn't this exactly what you taught me?" I asked, showing him what I thought were just new tweaks on his methodology.

He shook his head. "No, it isn't. I've never seen this before."

What had I done? I wasn't innovative—I knew that for a fact. I was just an ordinary team-building consultant.

Except, apparently, I wasn't. Apparently, I had created something really different. I needed to give it a name and develop it to its fullest potential. I called it "Agreements for Excellence."[1]

I went back to reading books and publications. After being away from them for over two years, however, I discovered that many of their logical methodologies and practices didn't reflect how the typically *illogical* human being consistently responds. My criterion for validating any new management book or keynote speaker was no longer how inspiring they were, but how accurately they reflected the human condition, with all its natural and innocent flaws and idiosyncrasies.

I didn't realize it at the time, but I had started on the journey to creating the B State transformation for business, culture, and individuals.

---

1   As I improved and expanded the process, I eventually renamed it "Rapid Team Results."

3

Raising Consciousness

*You can't drive to your destination
staring into the rearview mirror.*

–MARK SAMUEL

It took me two marriages to realize that analyzing past mistakes and break-downs had made me an expert—at what didn't work.

I had already discovered that when a client's team rehashed conflicts and people problems, those issues intensified. When they focused on what wasn't working and overanalyzed breakdowns, more problems surfaced. When they were asked to share their feelings, they always talked about whatever was happening *right then*—or, sometimes, about what they didn't like in the past.

I knew all that.

I knew, too, that constantly reviewing past mistakes reinforces the thinking, behaviors, and actions that got you where you are now, but I always remembered Einstein warning, "We can't solve problems by using the same kind of thinking we used when we created them." Focusing on the past can cement the idea that transformation is difficult and time consuming. It can even make you question your ability to change.

It certainly made me question mine.

Before my marriages, I made lists of my values, attributes, interests, desires, and needs so I could "scientifically" find my "best match." I knew exactly what I wanted from my ideal marriage. And the process led me to marry two great women.

Neither of them was my long-lasting, "best match" partner.

I worked hard on my own improvement during those two marriages, not only for myself, but to better my relationship with my then-wife. Even today, my rapport with both ex-wives couldn't be better. We all still support each other and consider ourselves family and best friends.

But neither marriage worked. None of us felt connected to our ideal loving partner.

Would I—*could* I—ever find and attract my perfect-match loving partner? After my second divorce, I didn't think I had much chance for that kind of happiness. I was damaged goods: frustrated, weary, and angry. Here I taught communication skills and team building, yet my personal life was a complete failure because of my flawed communication in my own relationships! Even though I could build teams with others outside my home, I had trouble building teamwork in my marriages.

I was stuck.

So I did exactly what Tom of Milstun Corporation did—only instead of hiring traditional change-management experts and running team-building workshops, I saw therapists and went to personal relationship–building workshops.

All of these were as useful for my marriages as they were for Tom's team—not at all.

Then, just as someone recommended that Tom call me, a friend recommended I call Aleya Dao, a unique life coach. She had no special credentials or certifications—just as I had no special validation for my methodology—but somehow she made me feel completely understood.

"What would it *feel like* to be with your ideal partner?" she asked. "I'm not talking about what she would look like or what her values or interests would be. I want you to think about what her energy and behavior would *feel* like. What would she do or say to make you feel *safe* when you got upset? How would she support you when you achieved a success? How would she make you feel *valued* for helping around the house instead of feeling like, once again, you haven't done enough?"

I blinked a few times. I had no idea what she was talking about—but I did suddenly understand why my teams always have a deer-in-the-headlights reaction when I ask similar questions in our initial meetings.

"Well," Aleya said with a laugh, "try it this way: You've had a hard day at work. What will she do or say to make you feel loved and supported? Will she give you space—or will she hold you? What will she do to help you calm down without making things worse?

"Let's flip that around. Suppose you had a great day—you got a promotion or achieved a big win. What reaction will she have that will make you feel honored or proud of your accomplishment?

"And what about day-to-day living? How will she make shopping or eating out or just visiting friends or family a fun thing to do as a couple?"

Aha! I got it!

I tore up my lists and started picturing and *feeling* my ideal partner's *energy* as she comforted me when I felt lonely. When I shared a success. When I was undecided or confused or angry.

It was amazing! My self-esteem, confidence, and satisfaction grew with each exercise. I got to the point where my relationship with *me* felt so good I didn't think I even needed another person in my life. I was my *own* soul mate.

A month later, I met someone who matched the "energy" of my imagination. She didn't have the background, career, or look I'd previously focused on, but I felt really good when we were together.

So did she.

We married two years later.

And our relationship keeps getting better and better.

We both still feel as if we're on a perpetual honeymoon. We love, adore, and appreciate each other more every day. Unlike my previous marriages, where I had to fight for safety or the need to be "right," our conflicts never last more than a couple of hours. When friction arises—maybe every two or three months—we first work on getting *ourselves* back into balance so we can both feel *safe* opening a conversation with each other. We openly share disagreements, but we *use* our conflicts to better understand our differences. Yes, we occasionally experience setbacks—who doesn't?—but our mutual commitment to our joint Picture of Success always gets us back on track quickly.

We created a B State marriage.

Release, Feel, Act

I would rather have a mind opened by wonder
than one closed by belief.

—Gerry Spence

This process for successful change is always the same, and really only works in this sequence, whether we're talking about our personal life, our budding enterprise, or our multinational organization that needs centralization.

First, we have to let go of our past failures, expectations, and self-admonishments. Second, we need to *feel* our future ideal, our emotionally satisfying Picture of Success. Finally, we must take whatever action is necessary to move rapidly toward that new reality.

Release the past, feel the future, make it happen.

That's the B State transformation formula that let me find my perfect mate, that led Tom's organization to centralization well within his board's deadline, and that can help bring about . . . whatever change you need to make in your life, with your team, or throughout your organization.

4

Becoming a Lifelong Student

*The beautiful thing about learning is
nobody can take it away from you.*

—B. B. KING

Schoolwork didn't come easily for me. I was a B student, and I had to work for those grades. I never considered myself a great student, even when I went to university for my bachelor's and master's degrees. For me, school was a means to an end. I couldn't wait to stop being a student and get a job.

I wanted to be comfortable and rest on my degrees.

When I got into the workplace, I knew I was prepared to be an expert based on my educational instruction and knowledge. I was perfectly ready for one of my first assignments: a very-tight-deadline project given to me by my CEO.

I knew I only had two months to get what really should have been a three-month project ready to present to a government agency in Sacramento, California.

I knew I had no resources of my own.

But I also knew—in my school-based logic—that if I needed any help, I had the right to use the resources around me. After all, this project was for the CEO!

So I went to three of the vice president's assistants and asked them to help me, in exchange for pizza. I'd buy.

Naturally, they all said, "Sure!"

I took them and the pizza up to a conference room on the second floor, and we nailed the project. I was thrilled. For once, I was going to turn in exactly what was expected—exactly on time.

I felt like a hero.

It never occurred to me that their bosses—and mine—had no idea where we all were. The next day, all three vice presidents called me into an office to confront me for "stealing" their assistants.

At first, I thought they were joking.

They weren't. They were really angry. I had crossed a line that I hadn't known existed.

I was scheduled to present the results of this two-month project to my CEO on a Thursday. That Wednesday—just one day before my appointment—I happened to run into her in the hallway.

"By the way," she said, "let me know if you need any help or resources to complete that project."

What!

"It's finished! I thought I had to deliver tomorrow! Why did you give me a hard deadline if there was no actual urgency?"

"Well, because no one completes their assignments on time. I figured you'd be late, like everybody else."

That doesn't make any sense. This isn't anything like school!

When will I know enough not to make mistakes from not knowing enough?

I was just out of grad school, but in my innocence I wanted to already be comfortable enough with my knowledge and experience to not make mistakes. Those feelings always seemed to elude me. I hadn't yet learned there would always be more I had to learn!

I'd forgotten that as a little boy of four or five, I loved to learn. I would pretend I was an adult. I had "play" adult conversations. I was an astronaut, a fireman, and a policeman. I wanted to learn everything: to ride a bike, to swim, to play ball. I never cared when I made mistakes.

Learning was fun!

But as I got older, comparing myself to others contaminated that fun. I didn't want to disappoint my parents, my teachers, or even my friends, who all seemed to judge everything I did. I learned to judge myself, too—even more harshly than everyone else did.

And so, learning stopped being exciting and fun. It became an almost painful chore.

We're all meant to continue learning, growing, and expanding through-out our lives—it's supposed to be a lifelong condition for humans. After all, the world continues to change and evolve; life never stays the same. We're constantly confronted with new challenges on all levels: physically, mentally, emotionally, societally, politically, financially, and even spiritually. We always have two choices: we can become ever more fearful with each new challenge or change, or we can use those experiences to grow stronger, gain greater perspective and awareness, and help others.

Ultimately, I realized my expertise comes from always remaining a student, always staying in a learning mode. It isn't comfortable, and there is always more to learn, but it keeps me in the game of exploration, expansion, and transformation.

I am never done growing. Neither are you.

Comfort Stunts Growth

Twenty years of experience, or one year
of experience repeated twenty times?

–Leandro Herrero

Life is a paradox.

We all want to feel comfortable in our relationships, at our jobs, and with our health—but, at the same time, we also want to continually experience greater loving, peace, and joy. And those two aspirations are in direct conflict. The process of growth and improvement—taking risks, making changes, learning new skills, letting go of past mistakes—is uncomfortable. Yet being comfortable means being complacent, and complacency doesn't allow for growth or change or improvement.

Once again, we're stuck.

Stuck in a bad relationship. Stuck in an unfulfilling job. Stuck with bad personal habits that injure our health.

"When we finally get sick and tired of being sick and tired, we will make the necessary change," said the author and public speaker John-Roger Hinkins.

But will we? Changing gets harder the more we resist—and the more time we waste trying to avoid the change, the stronger our resistance becomes.

Organizations face the same issues when they need to change and evolve—and they always have. I heard the following story decades ago:

Before computers became ubiquitous, management enrolled the senior clerical staff at a top California university in a training program to transition them from electronic typewriters to word processors. But the clerical pool banded together to resist going to the program: "We're incredibly effective on our typewriters. Why should we waste our time on these new-fangled machines?"

Management, in its attempt to keep its employees comfortable and happy, bent to their will. No one went to the training program.

By the end of the year, the university replaced all its typewriters with computers—and fired the entire clerical staff.

In another example, a billion-dollar corporation continued recording all their sales manually, years into the twenty-first century, because management couldn't agree on the "perfect" electronic system. Consequently, they couldn't effectively track their inventory, and their staff used work-arounds when they couldn't figure out the proper item number. They couldn't do any analytics on their sales to leverage their resources—so they didn't adjust to the market fast enough; they lost their competitive edge and stunted their own growth.

Comfort stunts employees' growth and can make them obsolete—but management's comfort stunts the organization's growth and can put it out of business.

Comfort Doesn't Create Psychological Safety

Sloppy success is better than perfect mediocrity.

—Alex Mandossian

In the ultrafast-paced twenty-first century, examples of resistant employees, managers, owners, and companies are too numerous to count. That's one reason why managers want their employees to feel comfortable. They want them to like their jobs, to feel good about their organization, and to get along with and respect their boss. They want people to feel a sense of autonomy within their own work space: they can decorate their area any way they want; they can solve their own problems; they can express themselves in their own style.

Even when someone doesn't perform, managers still want to make them feel comfortable. No one wants to upset someone else or cause a conflict, so at first they say nothing, hoping the employee will discover and correct their own mistakes.

Ensuring employee comfort is a high priority in many organizations.

If the employee's performance continues to decline, the manager finds ways to have repeated conversations about the issue rather than actually take corrective action. In large organizations, managers may get so frustrated that they transfer their nonperformer to another department, so it becomes another manager's headache.

In smaller organizations, the entrepreneur will opt to hire a COO to take care of the problems rather than accept that some people just aren't working out in the company—or that they, themselves, need to change, which is even more uncomfortable.

Welcome to bureaucracy!

Few managers or supervisors want to take the drastic step of letting an employee go. I've even seen nonperforming managers promoted to higher management positions just so their superiors can avoid any unpleasant changes. Besides, "He was a good guy."

I've seen this resistance go to ridiculous extremes. A manufacturing plant had to institute new safety procedures because people were getting hurt too often. The employees, of course, resisted the change, as people always do, but despite their complaints, the plant managers decided physical safety was more important than any temporary discomfort. They knew people would accept the new procedures as soon as they realized people weren't getting hurt so often.

Unfortunately, the corporate office coincidentally ran a "climate survey" to assess employee satisfaction at approximately the same time.

The employees, of course, expressed their dissatisfaction with the safety procedures by giving management low scores. Corporate, upset by the employees' discomfort, instructed the plant's management to start "responding and listening to your employees"—which meant reversing the safety procedures!

Yes, you read that right: the organization actually put employee comfort above physical safety.

Isn't that absurd? Talk about being stuck!

Uncontrollable Circumstances

> I prefer to march boldly in the direction of my dreams rather than to shrink in the shadows of my circumstances.
>
> –Michael Nila, founder, Blue Courage

As much as management wants to keep people comfortable rather than alter the status quo, they cannot control the drivers behind organizational change: competitive threats, customer demands, technological advancements, a declining economy, new government regulations—the list is endless. Companies have to be flexible to stay in business and grow.

But, just like in personal situations, organizations as a whole often initially react with denial and resistance. People get angry; they criticize anything different as "unnecessary" or "the wrong move" that will "lead to disaster." What's more, "The whole thing is unfair"—a mind-set that quickly enrolls others into a "victim" story.

Consequently, organizations more dedicated to people's comfort than to their growth often choose to slow down the change. They set up task forces to further analyze the situation. They engage employees with the hope of gaining their buy-in. They hire outside advisors and consultants to "do an assessment" and "make recommendations" that almost always end up reiterating what they already know.

But the uncontrollable circumstances don't care about anyone's feelings or resistance. They just keep on coming until the person or company is in so much pain they have to change to survive in the new reality.

Ironically, the enemy here is not the discomfort of the change. The enemy is denial and resistance, because change is actually a road map to freedom, liberation, and self-actualization.

Think about the last time you underwent a major personal transformation. Didn't you gain a new perspective on life? Didn't it add to your sense of well-being or confidence? Now think about this: Just before everything changed for the better, was your life going smoothly and easily? Or had you been brought to your knees by a challenge that made you question how you would survive?

Pretransformation pain comes from an instinctive fear of change or uncertainty. But not all pain is bad. Pain caused by the realities of life—not from abuse or punishment or someone's judgment—is "clean" pain. It's just life. So when we face rather than resist it, we almost always experience a positive transformation that wakes us up to new perspectives; and that awareness leads to greater innovation, creativity, personal growth, peace, and joy.

When we do things to make people "comfortable" rather than allow them to experience the transformative struggles of life—whether at work or at home—we rob them of the opportunity to gain greater competency, develop their self-confidence, and learn to navigate life's challenges better. In fact, having the goal of making people comfortable is like issuing a death sentence, one that leads them to become obsolete as they hold on to old paradigms, antiquated skills, and an inflexibility to change as the world around them continues to evolve and grow.

The underlying problem is, frankly, a basic misunderstanding of life, which impacts organizations, families, and even casual relationships. The truth is, comfort does not lead to excellence. It leads to complacency and sets people up for disappointment and failure whenever a real-life change comes along to disrupt their contentment.

Yet today's organizations—and parents and teachers and government—are obsessed with making people feel happy and secure. While it is true that people don't perform well when they're dissatisfied or unhappy, it's *not* true that happiness fosters high performance. They may do better than when they're miserable, but that doesn't mean they actually do well enough to generate better results.

I worked with an organization in a tight-knit rural community where everyone had grown up together, socialized together, and generally thought of each other as friends or extended family.

When they got to work, however, they didn't function well together at all.

They couldn't iron out conflicts or solve problems—they swept any issues under the rug so no one got upset. The company's operating costs were high; its efficiencies and customer-satisfaction ratings were low; and morale was mediocre.

But they were all friends!

That was the problem: they were all so friendly, they *couldn't* be accountable to each other—or to the organization—because their lifelong focus had always been on maintaining close community relationships.

I see this in varying degrees everywhere I go. One company I worked with thought the way to change their culture was to take everyone out for drinks every Friday night! Senior management even reprimanded one of their highest-functioning vice presidents because, even though she had great relationships with her staff, she *didn't* take her people out for happy hour every week.

Organizations are so focused on comfort, they get themselves into financial and operating trouble because no one actually feels safe enough to surface and address real issues. This sets up a destructive cycle, because when things get bad enough that leadership is backed into a corner and *must* do something to save the organization, they resort to drastic changes that so disrupt everyone's comfort, the employees feel "punished."

The managers lay people off. They restructure. They bring in consultants who dramatically cut resources and impose new procedures, policies, and benchmarks.

And while all this is happening and everyone is utterly panicked and stressed to the max, management reassures select people that—if they make it through all this—they'll get to be comfortable again after the change is completed. Promise.

So the cycle begins anew.

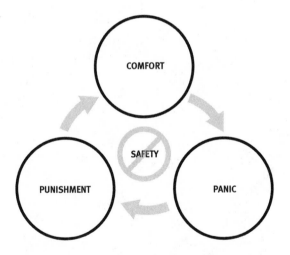

Figure 3: The Comfort-Panic-Punishment Cycle

This is no way to run a business. Or a family. Or a life.

Effective or innovative change never occurs during periods of comfort or punishment. It just cannot happen.

5

Safe Environments for Growth, Expansion, and Evolution

Risk more than others think is safe.
Care more than others think is wise.
Dream more than others think is practical.
Expect more than others think is possible.

−CLAUDE T. BISSELL

Rather than make people feel comfortable, we need to make them "safe" to risk change. What's the difference? Where comfort involves maintaining the status quo, a safe environment empowers people to face the unknown.

We rarely risk possible failure, embarrassment, or mistakes when we're comfortable. We certainly won't "take more initiative" or "be more innovative" when our micromanager punishes us for errors or deviations from their way of doing things. That kind of environment makes it more important to be comfortable than to try making anything work better.

But we will risk experimentation, float innovative ideas, and tell the truth—even if it's unpopular—when we're in a safe environment. Safety allows us to accept new techniques, try new communication tactics, and tolerate the normal ebb and flow of learning curves, with their built-in slower pace and occasional mistakes.

A safe environment lets people ask questions to gain understanding, resolve confusion, or raise concerns without being ridiculed or told, "You're not supporting the change!" It lets people support each other, learn and act, surface challenges during implementation, and solve problems together.

In a safe environment, people are acknowledged for the progress they're making and for sharing their best practices. It's seldom comfortable, but it can be fun and uplifting.

Improving Morale during Layoffs

How you relate to the issue, is the issue.

–Ron and Mary Hulnick

Nothing is less comfortable than when an organization must downsize. Morale bottoms out. Everyone's scared or angry or upset—or all three.

It's the same feeling as when we lose a parent or a spouse or, God forbid, a child. Nothing is okay, and we cannot see how it will ever be okay again.

I was brought in to help improve morale at an organization downsizing about 20 percent of its workforce. It seemed a strange request, as morale naturally drops when people fear losing their jobs. I thought their anger about their situation was perfectly reasonable, especially since it manifested in all the typical ways. Some people got into major verbal fights with their peers. Others simply "checked out" and didn't bother completing their work, which caused breakdowns for those still trying to serve customers. Even though some managers would also be laid off, management and employees became polarized. The environment grew toxic and painful.

How could I make anyone comfortable with such a negative situation? Those whose jobs were secure felt not only guilty, but stressed—they knew they'd soon have to do three people's work.

I knew change had to start with a different mind-set and habit of response. I also knew I'd have to modify the B State approach to address the current negativity, because it's not the demanding situation that gets people upset; it's the way they perceive and *react* to that situation.

The company didn't bring me in before things went sour—they didn't think about fixing things until they were already thirty days into the three-month layoff period—so I began by telling one group of very angry and distraught people the truth.

"The company will do more downsizing over the next two months, and there's nothing I can do about that. Some of you will be laid off—and there's nothing you or I can do about that, either. So, you each have a decision to make: you can stay angry about the change and keep taking your frustrations out on each other—which will just make this change all the more difficult and unpleasant for everyone—or you can support each other through it. Your choice."

No one said a word. They all looked shocked that I would propose this choice. Then one person spoke up.

"Do you think we can support each other through this mess, for real?"

"I don't know," I said with perfect honesty. "It would be an experiment. What I *do* know for sure is if you keep blaming management and exacerbating all the negativity in this situation, you will keep being miserable. In that case, you don't need my help—you've already nailed upset and anger—so we'll call this meeting over. On the other hand, if you decide to support each other, I'll stay and guide you through creating a supportive environment."

I stopped talking, sat down, and waited. And waited. And waited. I knew they had to choose their own empowerment and ownership without me encouraging them to do what I thought best. Finally, someone said, "I guess we have nothing to lose. Let's see what it means to support each other."

Good! "So," I asked the group, "what would you need to do differently to support each other through the layoff period?"

"We need to accept that different people will have different reactions during the transition," one person offered, "and we need to honor those responses."

I wrote that on the flip chart. "What do the rest of you think?"

"We need to stay focused on our job and support those who are struggling that day."

I wrote that down, too. They didn't know it, but we were creating a B State Team Agreement.

"If someone loses their job," a third person said, "we'll all use our networks to help them find a new one."

I felt the energy of the group begin to shift and relax a little.

"Sometimes, I need to vent my emotions and frustrations," someone else said. "I just need to let off steam."

"Okay," I said, "but there have to be some guidelines. You can only choose one person as a sounding board, and you must ask permission for a one-minute venting period during which you can express anything freely—with any language—without fear of judgment or repercussion. Afterward, you *must* go back to work."

Everyone applauded.

Someone raised a hand. "In the past, when I got restructured into a new team, my old team cut me off from social events and information sharing. I felt abandoned. That made everything harder, because I'd lost my old team but hadn't yet been accepted into my new one. I couldn't afford to quit—and my wife said I should just be thankful I still had a job. But I was miserable for a long time."

"Let's add that condition," I said as I wrote. "If anyone is transferred to another department, the team will stay connected and include them in regular social activities."

"We need more information from management to prevent rumors and keep us from feeling helpless and out of the loop about what's happening," someone put in, carefully not looking at the management-team leader in the room.

"How about this?" the leader responded. "Let's have a five-to-ten-minute get-together every morning so I can keep you up to date about what's going on and address any rumors you may have heard."

"That'll be okay," said a team member, "*if*, at the get-together, we can also ask for some support without being blamed or ridiculed. I know some of us just need to be left alone, but sometimes a little conversation, or even a hug of reassurance, would be an immense help."

By the time we completed the B State Team Agreement, everyone felt they had a safety net to get through the next two months. More upbeat and at ease, they formally documented the agreement. They got together to review it each week, and as they each felt their teammates' support, morale rose. Later, near the end of the layoffs, one team member told me, "Our morale is higher now than it ever was, even before the downsize. We've never been so supportive of each other. There were always cliques and blame-game fights between people. Now we support each other emotionally, and we're performing better than ever! We don't have the breakdowns and communication problems we used to have. When there's a problem, no one is afraid to talk about it, so we resolve it instead of letting it fester. And our last customer-service scores actually went up!"

I was delighted, of course, especially since I got similar reports from all the teams we worked with during the downsizing. I've since been asked to create the same kind of safe environment in numerous other companies—in many countries and cultures—as they, too, went through the discomfort of downsizing and restructuring, whether as the result of economic conditions or acquisition.

B State Team Agreements

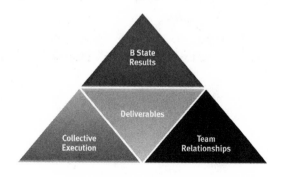

Figure 4: B State Implementation Model

Courage starts with showing up
and letting ourselves be seen.

–Brené Brown

Building trust, support, and effective communication is not a one-size-fits-all process. The Gen Z "mass personalization"—individualized products and identifications on a massive commercial level—recognizes how we're all individuals with unique needs, beliefs, and behaviors that cannot simply be narrowed down to sixteen styles or other forms of typecasting. The B State, too, recognizes that most people will never accept or adhere to generic team guidelines and core values. That's why every B State Team Agreement must be unique for its specific team and based solely on everyone's needs in relation to the team.

Ergo, those Team Agreements will change over time as teams and members evolve.

A twenty-person extended-management team had low scores in trust, communication, and decision-making. I clearly recognized the problem after observing just one meeting: five people did all the talking while the others remained silent, and everyone was upset about it. The five resented the others for not speaking up, and the others resented the five for dominating every discussion.

"What can you do differently to ensure better team communication in your meetings?" I asked the group.

"Every team member needs to commit to *voluntarily* share their ideas and opinions on every discussion in our meetings so no one dominates, and everyone feels heard," one of the five said.

"That's a big commitment," I said, writing his statement on the flip chart. "Does everyone else agree this is a good idea for your team?"

"Yes," several people responded simultaneously.

"It's the only way we can ever change this team's dynamic," one of the fifteen quiet members said.

"What will you each—individually—need to feel safe enough to share your ideas openly in team meetings?"

"No put-downs or attacks for what we say," a second "quiet" member offered.

"Openly listen to each other without judgment before responding," said a third.

As they all individually shared their concerns or needs, I added them to the agreement in a separate "Conditions for Acceptance" section.

"If you're going to openly listen to people's ideas and input, what do you need in order to make sure this is practical for you and your team?"

"Stay on topic rather than move to tangents."

"Don't go on and on repeating yourself over and over again!"

The entire team cracked up in laughter.

"Okay, good work, everybody," I said. "We need to take our afternoon break. When we come back, we'll complete the agreement."

Ann pulled me aside during the break. "Can I talk to you?" she asked. "I really like this agreement and process, but . . . I'm extremely shy. I can't keep to this agreement as it's written in good faith. Can you bring this up for me when we go back?"

"I understand your concern," I said, "but if you think about it, you'll see why I can't surface this for you. You have to do it yourself."

She looked down and shook her head.

"What I can do," I hurried on, "is help you to surface this with the group. I'd be happy to do that."

She smiled. "Okay!"

I kicked off the after-break discussion: "Ann has something she wants to share with all of you."

Ann shot daggers at me with her eyes. Okay, that wasn't very nice—but after taking a deep breath, she did manage to say, "As you all know, I am . . . very shy and . . . introverted. This agreement says we will *volunteer* our ideas and input—I . . . I can't do that."

When no one responded to her, I asked, "Can you still have this agreement but make an exception for Ann?"

Bill turned to her. "If we want your idea or opinion, can we call on you to share it with us openly?"

"Yes! Absolutely! I totally commit to sharing openly—just not voluntarily."

"Then I'm okay with those conditions," Bill said. "What about the rest of you?"

Everyone agreed. Like most people, they hadn't realized agreements need not be uniform or boilerplate. The team could make exceptions for individuals without relinquishing the agreement's intent.

The manager, one of the five "speakers," said, "You know what? This is the first time I've seen true diversity demonstrated—not by race, religion, or country of origin, but individually, based on us all being unique. This is a real demonstration of support."

When an issue was surfaced at our follow-up session six months later, sixteen of the twenty team members actively and openly shared—quite an improvement from the original five. They were at the next development stage, where they wasted time in endless debate. That's the natural human growth process; solving one problem creates the next higher level of problems. I was about to make this a learning moment when Ann slammed her hand on the table and stood up.

"We're going around in circles!" she shouted. "We're not getting anywhere! We all need to take a breath!"

I looked around expecting everyone to be as shocked as I was by this shy, introverted woman's outburst, but they all just sat quietly.

"Did anyone notice anything peculiar about what just happened?" I prodded.

Everyone looked at me in silence.

"Didn't anyone notice Ann's behavior?"

Still no response.

"You had an agreement that Ann wouldn't volunteer her opinion until asked," I pointed out. "Yet she just slammed her hand on the table and shouted at all of you."

"Oh, yeah," one team member said. "Heck, Ann stopped needing that condition three months ago. Now we can't keep her quiet. She talks all the time."

I was the one who learned a lesson that day: when people create a truly "safe" environment, they can evolve past their previous labels, styles, and inhibitions to participate with greater courage and confidence. Forming B State Team Agreements isn't about following the rules. It's about learning how to create a safe environment, so people can evolve to higher levels of trust, support, and transparency.

Families Need Safety Too

> Trust is the glue of life. It's the most essential
> ingredient in effective communication. It's the
> foundational principle that holds all relationships.
>
> —Stephen Covey

A friend asked me to facilitate a B State Team Agreement with his family. He was frustrated that his teenage son and daughter acted out during dinners at home, during family get-togethers, and when asked to do chores.

I started by asking each person, "What is one thing you'd like to see changed in your family's expectations and communications?"

"I want more cooperation and participation in family activities from my son and daughter," Dad started off.

"I want less fighting and yelling," Mom stated.

"What do you guys want?" I asked the kids.

"I want more time with my friends," Megan said.

"I want to be left alone to play my video games," Tommy shared.

On the flip chart, I wrote:

Each family member contributes to the togetherness of the family and supports each person's individual interests in a balanced manner while effectively communicating and listening without shouting.

"Do you agree with this basic statement?" I asked.

"Yeah," Megan said, "but we don't know *how* to do that."

"That's okay for now. What do you think is a reasonable time for family contribution, and how do you think it should work?"

"I think we should get to split our time for dinners fifty-fifty, so we sometimes eat together and sometimes eat with our friends," Megan said. "And we should have set times for doing chores so we can plan when we can be with our friends ahead of time."

I wrote down those conditions for acceptance. "Anybody else?"

"I'm okay with what Megan said," Tommy put in, "but if I'm in the middle of a game, I want to finish it before coming to the table."

"Wait a minute," Mom interrupted. "I don't want dinner to get cold. I think we should have a set time for dinner and *you* plan *your* time to be there."

"I guess that's okay," Megan said. "If it's really going to be the same time every day instead of whenever Dad gets home. Tommy?"

"Okay, I can agree with that."

"But I can't get home at the same time every day," Dad protested.

"We all understand that, but I think the three of us need more consistency at this point," Mom said. "And if we schedule dinner for 6:30 every night, you'll make it three out of five nights—and when you can't, you'll know we've already eaten and will have to make do with leftovers."

"All right, I can go along with that," Dad said. "But what frustrates me is that no one listens when they're called."

"Instead of voicing your frustration," I put in, "what do you want, and what do you think is reasonable?"

"Sometimes I can't get Megan or Tommy's attention when I want to talk to them about something. I want them to listen and help me out if I need them. Right then. Not later."

"What do you think about that?" I asked the kids.

"If it isn't at a scheduled time," Megan said to her father, "then I'm probably doing something else, so *you're* interrupting *me*. I think I should be able to finish whatever I'm doing before I have to respond."

"Do you think that's reasonable?" I asked Dad.

"I suppose—but you could at least let me know you heard me and how much time you need before I can get your attention."

"What do you guys think?" I asked. "Is that reasonable?"

"Okay," Megan said. "I'll commit to telling you I'm busy and when I'll be available."

"Me too," Tommy agreed.

"But we all make mistakes," Mom put in. "What can we do so we don't end up fighting and yelling?"

"Great question!" I said. "What are you going to do *differently* when you get frustrated?"

No one answered. This is where they got stuck.

"Let me offer a suggestion," I said, "and you can massage it afterward. Since this is a change for everyone, let's not expect perfection. How about if you all commit to a once-a-week family meeting at one of your family dinners to review this agreement and discuss whenever anyone felt a lack of cooperation. You'll either get back to the agreement as it is, or work together to resolve whatever caused the problem. If you break the agreement, you'll voluntarily admit you messed up—and that's particularly important for you two, Mom and Dad. You're the ones who create or destroy the safety. No one needs to be in this alone. You're a great family. You can work out your differences together. How does that sound to everybody?"

Everyone was excited about a weekly family meeting except for Tommy—but he did agree to support everyone else.

"You just have to include one more condition," I said. "No yelling—okay, Dad?"

"Fine, I won't yell—but only if we all keep to this agreement!"

"Good. But yelling is an old, ingrained habit for you, so what can they say or do that won't set you off even more—if you start getting louder and more intense?"

"Just say, 'Hey, you're getting intense; take a breath,' and I promise to bring it down."

"Promise?" Mom asked.

"Yeah, yeah."

I reviewed the agreement with every condition and asked each person to give their commitment. They all said yes and looked much more positive and relaxed than when we first sat down.

When I checked in with them three months later, they had figured out that just keeping to the agreement wasn't what made things work—it was what happened when someone *didn't* keep their commitment that mattered. They didn't yell, blame, fight, or hide. When schedules changed, they modified their "family time" together. And they were all much better about owning up to their mistakes and giving and receiving forgiveness.

They had become a B State family.

6

Optimizing Energy

People who say it cannot be done
should not interrupt those who are doing it.

—CHINESE PROVERB

No one ever uses the word "energy" to describe their work environment. Yet even though we can't see it, measure it, or control it, we experience or feel it every day.

We get a lot done on those days when everything vibrates at a high level, whether it's a project at work, cleaning the house, or even shopping. We're in sync with what we're doing, in tune with ourselves and our surroundings, so we experience grace and ease as we pursue and achieve our goals. We feel unstoppable.

Then there are the days when we wake up feeling sluggish. We hit the snooze button—three or four times—before we can force ourselves out of bed. Taking a shower and getting dressed are chores, and deciding what to eat for breakfast . . . forget about it! Our minds move slower and our brains feel mushy as we try to organize our day or accomplish even the most routine tasks. We feel clumsy. We stumble in meetings. We cannot figure out how to get the right words out of our mouth.

Other times, we feel overwhelmed by everything we need to do. Our energy fragments as we start and stop half a dozen different tasks or projects, hoping that if we put out enough energy in enough directions, at least *something* will get done. That's my worst nightmare—feeling under too much pressure as I bust my butt to get everything done and fall short on almost all of it.

Organizations also vibrate with these different energies. It feels so good when we're working with a high-flying, positive, focused group that accomplishes a lot, communicates well, and provides excellent customer service. People laugh and joke rather than complain under their breath or struggle to hold in their temper. It's downright fun.

But in an organization mired in bureaucracy, territorial silos, micromanagement, and an overall sense of victimization, the energy is sluggish, and everything feels like a chore. Even a normal workload feels overwhelming. Instead of using what little energy is available to get things done, it gets squandered on blaming, infighting, and endless debates.

Low Energy Is Stuck Energy

> Anyone can make the simple complicated.
> Creativity is making the complicated simple.
>
> –Charles Mingus

I had a government job while I worked for my master's degree. My boss, the executive director, handed me a project with a supertight deadline, one aspect of which was to photocopy a single five-page document. But it was the late seventies and few employees had free access to the office copy machine, so I couldn't just complete that simple task; I had to go through the copy-machine clerk.

"Good morning," I said, approaching her with a smile. "Can you please make a copy of this five-page document for me?"

She did not respond. I know she heard me—she was right there at her desk, facing me as she read a novel and ate a snack.

Maybe it's her break time. I'll wait until she's back.

Actually, I had no choice but to wait, since she controlled who went in and out of the copy-machine room.

So I waited.

After a few minutes, I said cheerfully, "I'm working on a project for the executive director, and it'd be great if you could help me make a copy of this document!"

"Sure," she said, still not looking up. "I'll make you a copy."

But she didn't move—or stop reading.

I hesitated a bit longer, then blurted out, "Is it possible to copy my document *now?*"

"I'm *getting* to it!" she snapped. "Making copies takes time!"

I glanced around—there were no piles waiting at the machine to be copied and nothing in her in-box.

"This is for the executive director!" I insisted.

"All right!" she said, slamming down her book. "I'll stop what *I'm* doing to get *your* copies made."

That was the moment I decided to never get a full-time position with the government. I had too much personal energy to wait out an enervated clerk's resistance to actually doing anything.

The Natural Flow Path

Energy constantly ebbs and flows around and through us, like ocean waves on the shore. Sometimes they crash, sometimes they merely roll, but they're always in motion.

We can add *resistance* to our personal energy flow when things are happening too fast and we want to slow down. We squeeze our bicycle's hand brakes, for example, turn our skis, or even take a step back from a relationship moving forward too fast. Our deliberate resistance prevents us from crashing, falling, or committing to something we're not ready for.

But when we're on level ground and squeeze the brakes while still pedaling, we make the work harder than it needs to be. That extra energy demand causes stress and confusion because resisting our own natural energy flow is ultimately exhausting. We get ourselves stuck without realizing what we're doing. We think we're just worried. Or concerned about looking bad to others. Or being self-critical because things haven't gone as expected. Or feeling overwhelmed or confused from having too much to do. Those kinds of roller-coaster reactions, with their built-in negative attitudes, induce procrastination—another resistance behavior—and keep us from being "present" in the moment, focusing on the next action, and moving forward.

Resistance is self-perpetuating; it feeds on itself. When we aren't moving forward, we naturally feel bad about ourselves. We should be doing better. We should be learning faster and getting results more quickly. We basically "should" ourselves into a tailspin of self-judgment, jealousy, self-doubt, and pity. Will we ever get it right or be good enough?

Probably not.

Could we be more stuck?

I remember when I had only three weeks left to hand in my article for my consulting company, IMPAQ's, first newsletter. I felt extremely anxious about my tardiness.

I'm a bad writer . . . and I hate writing.

I'd already procrastinated for two weeks trying to figure out the right approach to the article. I finally sat down and frantically wrote an outline, only to crumple it up and start a new one. I couldn't get it right.

"Just use *one* of your outlines and get started," my then-wife advised.

I tried, but my stress and frustration grew worse with each new draft I threw out in disgust. *I'm a complete failure! I wish someone would magically save me from this dreadful task!* I took showers so I could cry without anyone hearing me (while I got clean). My mind raced in so much despair I couldn't sleep.

All that resistance—procrastinating, going around in mental circles, trying to wish the job away—was so disruptive it completely paralyzed my natural flow.

"I give up," I finally told my wife. "I just can't do it."

"Oh, come on—give it one more try."

"No! I just don't have it in me! I feel completely beat up over this assignment!"

I grabbed a bag of tortilla chips and a Diet Coke and turned on an episode of *Seinfeld* to chill out. The show was so funny, ridiculous, and awkward, I stopped thinking about the article altogether and just laughed. Suddenly, out of nowhere, I "caught" a whisper of an approach at the back of my mind. It wasn't a loud "aha" moment—I easily could have missed it—but the more I thought about it, the more curious I became to see whether it could work.

I left the TV on and went to my office. I wasn't committed to writing anything—I just wanted to explore the new idea.

About ninety minutes later, I was back watching TV.

"What are you going to do about the article?" my wife asked as she passed through the room.

"Oh, it's done."

"What! When did that happen? I thought you'd given it up!"

"I actually emailed it to my teammate about fifteen minutes ago."

"I'm gonna kill you! After all you put me through this week, you just tossed it together and sent it off?"

"I guess when I stopped agonizing over it, the ideas simply came together. I got back in my natural flow."

My explanation didn't sit well with my wife, but it did make me realize I always have two choices when I get stuck: I can either opt for the old habit of getting ahead of myself and projecting an unavoidable negative outcome; or I can relax, distract myself, and let the answer come to me.

Teams have the same two choices about the resistances they throw up to impede their natural energy flow. They can complain, blame, and project disastrous scenarios; or they can step back, reassess, plan, cooperate, and take positive action.

An organization can also add unnecessary resistance to its natural, energetic flow of serving customers, expanding markets, and growing their business—

- It lets management and employees work against each other, blame, and finger-point, and make everyone feel too victimized to get anything done.

- It operates from a place of fear and resistance and thus wastes time persuading people to buy into its ideas rather than just move forward.

- It creates an unsafe environment for employees to offer innovative ideas and suggestions for improvement due to power plays and autocratic leaders' micromanagement.

- It falls into the paralysis of analysis to avoid decision-making, thus fostering procrastination and stalling forward movement.

- It allows favoritism, which prevents meaningful development and clear career paths for up-and-coming employees, supervisors, and managers.

- It couples unclear or low expectations with low accountability.

- It lacks the courage to address poor performers and attitudes, thereby causing work-arounds that reduce efficiency and effectiveness.

These behaviors and attitudes cannot be resolved by core values, strategic plans, additional metrics, process improvement, or training programs, because they are *accepted habits*, even though they foster perpetual frustration, inefficiency, wasted resources, and burnout. Yet, like artery blockages, they're sufficiently obstructive to cause organization disease and, ultimately, death.

Any organization truly dedicated to high performance, evolution, and customer loyalty must follow the natural energy flow that results when people with clear direction and expectations feel safe, engaged, and supported. I call it the "path of least resistance."

One Organization's Strategic Plan

A large family-owned Latin American business had achieved its success by letting its managers simply meet their numbers. No one expected improved performances. No one looked to develop future leaders. As long as each business unit and functional department met its metrics, business continued as usual.

Eventually, though, the CEO decided it was time for the company to improve processes and margins and reduce its dependency on people nearing retirement. Accordingly, the senior management team implemented a new strategic-planning process to identify what areas needed improvement and which potential leaders needed development. In most established organizations, that would have been a standard, ongoing process and would take about a month to document and share with others. But as this was a new concept for the company, the leaders were given a template and training and a month to produce a *rough draft*.

They spent that month complaining, resisting, and outright refusing to change.

"Why should I have to write all this stuff down?" several leaders demanded at the monthly meeting. "I know what I need to get done!"

"Based on our growth and the fact that many of you are reaching retirement within the next five years," the CEO responded, "we need consistent practices to guide our growth—practices that people who haven't been here for thirty-five years can easily understand and implement."

The leadership team spent the second month sorting out their confusion, since they'd forgotten what they were supposed to do based on the training they'd received two months earlier. Half of them completed their plans by the third-month meeting. The other half were "still working on it," so they spent the fourth month either fixing their completed plans based on the CEO's feedback, or getting individual coaching to overcome their confusion or difficulties with the assignment.

In the fifth-month meeting, resistance resurfaced, since everyone had already acted without a written plan and viewed the process as a waste of time. The ever-patient CEO explained the whys and wherefores once again, and insisted the plans be completed. The rest of that month went to correcting the remaining plans. When they were finally shared at the *sixth-month* meeting—halfway through the year!—team members found common projects they could work on together, and the energy level in the room shot up.

What a great idea this was! Why hadn't they done it a long time ago?

The Energy of a Problem Is Different from the Energy of a Solution

> Man [You] cannot discover new oceans unless he has
> [you have] the courage to lose sight of the shore.
>
> —André Gide

Remember a recent problem that took you a while to solve? Remember the feelings you had while you worked to find the solution—worry, anxiety, even self-doubt? Now recall how you felt when the solution finally occurred to you. Did you feel different? Were you suddenly more relaxed? Had you become distracted from the problem itself? Or had the solution woken you up in the middle of the night?

When we tackle a problem, our energy is usually constrained, restricted, and limited, but when we realize or come upon a solution, it's open, accepting, and curious. Generally, when we focus on problems, we get more problems—which was exactly what happened to me toward the end of my financial recovery, about one and a half years after the financial downturn of 2008 when I faced the possibility of bankruptcy.

I had started to make a good income, but I never *saw* it because I lived on a small monthly allowance while my accountant paid off my debts. Consequently, I was shocked when my tax bill was $75,000 over what I planned for. I hadn't set aside anywhere near that amount—and it was already August.

I freaked out. I immediately blamed the government for demanding so much money when I was living so frugally and paying off my debts.

Then I tried to figure out how to quickly earn an extra $75,000—to no avail.

I had nightmares about never getting out of debt. I grew depressed and anxious, just as I had when I originally faced the prospect of bankruptcy. I beat the drum of the problem and exhausted myself as fear, negativity, and useless remedies piled up.

Finally, my wife stepped in. "What's so wrong that you're freaked out?"

"I have an *unexpected* tax bill of *seventy-five thousand dollars*, and I have *no way* to pay it!"

"How much time do you have to come up with the money?"

"It's due in seven months!" I exclaimed, as anxious as if it were due the next day.

"Oh, hell no!" she said. "No way I'm going to live with this fearful attitude of yours for another six months. You have to get a hold of yourself. You know how to do this. Find a 'higher perspective' and trust that you'll be inspired with a solution. You have six months to save seventy-five thousand dollars. Figure it out!"

And she walked away.

Taken aback by her uncharacteristically strong response, I nevertheless knew she was right. I decided to use the "wonder" technique I'd learned from a coach and friend of mine. Any time I started to worry about the bill, I stopped and asked, "I wonder what the solution to this tax debt is?"

As I got dressed about a week later, I asked the question again. Out of nowhere, I saw an image of my published book.

"That's weird."

I continued dressing—and the image reappeared.

"Why is the book showing up in my consciousness?" I wondered aloud. My accountant's projected-client-income report suddenly came to mind. "Huh—what does one thing have to do with the other?" The book image showed up again and quickly turned into a cash-flow image.

"Aha! The money from my book can pay off my taxes!"

It was a simple solution. Book sales aren't predictable, so that revenue wasn't part of my company's predicted cash flow. I never planned to pay expenses with it.

"Do you think we can set aside enough money from book sales to pay the tax bill?" I asked my accountant.

"Based on how it's sold for the last six months, yes! What a great idea! How did you come up with it?"

"Actually, it just came to me. I didn't think of it, or brainstorm solutions, or use any problem-solving process. It just *came to me*."

It was indeed an "Aha!" moment. I suddenly realized that when families and organizations focus or talk about problems instead of solutions or ways to make things better, they generate negative energy that gets them—and keeps them—stuck.

Ignoring a problem because you don't want to be negative also takes a lot of energy—negative energy. "Don't think about your late project" creates the same effect as *thinking* about the late project. Doing affirmations about completing the project still keeps you focused on the project.

Every goal is two-sided: the desire for what you want, and the absence of it. "Unmentionables"—be they poor behavior or actions—get activated by focusing on *not* focusing on them. When we ignore but nevertheless get irritated by mediocre performance or behavior, we increase our negative energy. When we simply deal with the situation, we increase our positive energy. The key is to focus on the solution, not the problem, so avoid questions like these:

"Why are we still dealing with this breakdown?"

"Whose fault is it that we haven't resolved this problem yet?"

"Why is it taking you so long to make progress?"

"When do you expect this problem to get resolved?"

Instead, pose solution-oriented questions:

"What do you want the solution to accomplish?"

"What would people be doing differently if they focused on creating the ideal solution?"

"What would *you* do differently if the solution was already in place?"

The Problem-to-Solution Exercise

During the two-day B State Mastership program, we form participant groups of three and tell them to each write down three to five projects they've been avoiding.

"They can be personal projects, like clearing out the garage or decluttering your office, or work-related projects," I explain.

When everyone finishes, I ask, "Now . . . how do you feel?"

"Awful," someone usually says.

"Discouraged," and "Everything feels hard and stuck, like being in quicksand," others typically answer.

"No wonder you haven't made much progress," I console them. "Now choose the one project that makes you feel the most stuck and imagine you've already accomplished it super effectively. Take the next two minutes to describe to your two teammates what it looked and felt like as you did that. Be as detailed as possible. Include the support others gave you, how it was magically effortless, how you solved problems that arose during the process, and how you made good decisions. Meanwhile, your teammates cheer you on. They'll acknowledge your creativity, critical thinking, organization, and leadership as you relate your ideal story, so make it real! They'll also ask questions to help you disclose more details:

- How did you handle questions or any resistance that came up?
- How did you handle competing priorities that surfaced?
- What did you do to celebrate afterwards?

"Do we have time to plan what to say?" someone always asks.

"No! Just think about it being completed, and make up the story about how you did it with such grace and ease. Ready? Set? Go!"

The energy in the room always rises as people get into their success stories. After everyone in each group has shared their story and been cheered by their teammates, I ask, "How do you feel now?"

"Totally energized!"

"I feel so positive about my project!"

"I'm not afraid of this project anymore—I know exactly how to begin!"

"Fantastic!" I said. "But remember, in physical-world reality, you're no further along than you were ten minutes ago when you felt so discouraged. The project is still fully in front of you, but you've moved. By focusing on the solution rather than the problem, you've come up with ideas you never imagined before. As John-Roger Hinkins said, 'It's foolish to lose in your own fantasy.'"

B State companies always focus on and move toward their Picture of Success rather than continually reiterate what and who are broken. They foster a safe environment for open engagement at all levels, focus on replacing what hasn't worked with what will work, experiment with new approaches, and modify processes to optimize results. They maintain their attention on where they are going, remove any obstacles along the way, and innovate as they go.

The B State never gets stuck!

7

B State Energy

Remember, you and you alone are responsible
for maintaining your energy. Give up blaming, complaining
and excuse making, and keep taking action in the
direction of your goals—however mundane or lofty they may be.

—JACK CANFIELD

I sense or feel energy when I work with clients. I find it a very useful tool, and it comes across to me quite clearly and quickly, whether I'm dealing with an individual or a group.

I normally don't see it. The only time I did, it changed my life.

My ex-wife Nancy and I were having a discussion in our bedroom—not arguing or even debating, just sharing different points of view—when our four-year-old daughter barged into the room without knocking or verbal warning.

She was "charged" about something—and I *saw* her energy transfer to my wife like a bolt of lightning.

I was stunned. I was even more stunned when Nancy then turned to shout at me as if we were in one of our heated arguments!

Oh! This isn't her at all!

Instead of reacting and getting defensive like I normally did, I just stopped the conversation. "Sarah," I said, "can you give us some time to finish our conversation? Go back to your room, and we'll both be there in just a few minutes."

When she left, I asked Nancy, "How are you feeling about our conversation?"

"I'm really bothered by it!"

"But you didn't seem bothered before Sarah came in."

She hesitated. "Nooo . . . I wasn't."

"Did I do anything to upset you?"

"I can't think of anything."

I told her what I'd seen. "It was like you picked up on Sarah's energy and instantly got mad at me. It was amazing! I could see it wasn't your anger, it was hers."

"Wow," she said. "You're right. And frankly, I was confused by my sudden reaction. It seemed to come out of nowhere."

From that point forward, we started watching our reactions—especially our negative ones—to see whether we were being impacted by anyone else.

When my business started to grow a few years later, I hired two competent expert-in-their-field consultants. After about nine months, I noticed they had formed a very strong relationship and were demanding changes that didn't align with our business model. I also literally felt them whispering negative potshots to each other about me from the back of a large room, which disturbed and distracted me as I delivered an important presentation.

I hired an outside consultant to assess the situation. He spent about three months with our team, making it a point to closely observe the two consultants. Finally, he told me, "I've done my assessment."

"And . . . ?"

"And you're the problem!"

"I'm open to your counsel—what am I doing wrong?"

"You haven't fired them yet! You're the leader here, but they'll take you down if you don't get rid of them."

So I did—and I started giving credence to people's negative and positive energy flows. It was a bit tricky at first to sort out whether someone's reaction was theirs or the result of someone else's negativity, but over the years I've gotten better at making those distinctions. It all comes down to awareness and practice.

Energetic Preparation

Our personal energy impacts every goal we set, every plan we make, and every change we present. When we don't deliberately optimize our energy, we can throw up obstacles, generate misfires, or create confusion, even when our direction seems clear on paper. We all know *preparation* comes between planning and action, but while most of us prepare handout materials, PowerPoint slide shows, and recorded videos, we almost never do the "inner preparation" that readies us for *optimal performance*.

Professional athletes and musicians psych themselves up prior to every game and performance. Documentaries of Michael Jackson, Jennifer Lopez, and Kevin Hart, for example, show how they bring their entire group together to "center" themselves before they go onstage. Athletic teams often say a prayer together to get everyone aligned. Anthony Robbins goes through an entire routine of affirmations and physical activities to raise his energy level before stepping out in front of his audiences of thousands.

We seldom talk about these kinds of purpose-driven, energy-focused pep rallies in business, but they're just as necessary and effective. Elaine Vincent, executive director of the town of Okotoks in Alberta, Canada, delivered just such a "psych-up" speech to her team shortly before they had to implement a major operational change.

"We're under pressure to transform, based on our community's challenges," she told them. "We have a mission to serve our community the best we can. The changes ahead will require the highest level of focus, collaboration, and regular updates between and amongst you all. I see us aligned and supporting each other as we implement new processes so we're more responsive to our constituents. I know and trust that you will take the high road to solve problems and make decisions. We all need to be together at the top of the triangle. I'm excited about these changes and about your leadership to make them happen. We've created this plan together—now it's time to implement it in unison and harmony. Any questions?"

"We're ready!" one manager called out.

"Let's get this party started!" another spoke up.

"Fantastic!" Elaine said. "Let's make history!"

Action to Movement to Momentum

If you are offered a seat on a rocket ship,
don't ask what seat! Just get on.

–Sheryl Sandberg

Stage One: Action represents the initial steps we take on any new project, transformation, or forward movement. These steps are usually the hardest and least efficient, just as a rocket separating from the launchpad looks as if it's hardly moving. Runners know the first few steps off their blocks are the most difficult. It takes a lot of energy to get started on anything, especially when we feel we're not making a lot of progress in return. That's why beginnings so often turn into endings. With so little to show for all our laborious initial effort, it's easy to get frustrated and just quit.

"Why am I bothering?"

"Am I doing the right thing?"

"Will my *effort* really produce my desired *results*?"

"Will it even be worth the effort if I achieve what I'm trying to do?"

Beginnings are also the stage at which negativists, resisters, and deniers are the loudest.

"It'll never work!"

"You're wasting all our time and money!"

"Come on, we tried this before. Let's do it the way we know works."

Those concerns and questioning are thinly disguised efforts to resist change and stay in (or move back into) an A State. Their negative energy and fear cannot be overcome by more presentations, analyses, workshops, or other standard efforts to get them to "buy in," but they can sap other people's energies and create a "two steps forward/one step back" disruption. No wonder so many people give up during this early stage of change—be it a diet, an exercise regimen, a household chore, or an organizational transformation. They haven't had enough time to transform their mixed-energy patterns.

Overcoming the natural resistance to any beginning requires consistent and continual action fueled by positive energy. Should a problem arise, adjust and keep moving—over and over again. Don't stop too long to ensure everything is perfectly on course or to appease the negativists; any long pause will impede forward motion and undermine optimism. The change's rhythm will normalize with your consistent and continual action.

Sometimes thinking too much
can destroy your momentum.

–Tom Watson

Stage Two: Movement indicates a greater harmony and cooperation between you and your efforts to achieve your desired outcome. "Two steps forward/one step back" transforms into "every step forward/no steps back." The runner is already a quarter of the way around the track and doesn't need as much effort to keep going. You're a few weeks into your exercise/diet regimen and no longer think about setting aside time to work out or eat properly. In an organization, people complete their assignments, communicate with each other freely, and resolve breakdowns when they surface.

It takes three to six months to progress from Action to Movement after our two-day B State transformation program unless the team experiences a sense of urgency that shortens the time frame or a crisis that derails the progress.

At **Stage Three: Momentum**, every step moves you *three* steps forward. Momentum makes it literally *hard to stop*, just as Newton's first law of motion states: an object in motion tends to remain in motion. The runner can't simply stop once she's passed the finish line; she must consciously slow down or collapse. The dieter/exerciser finds she resists earlier eating and sedentary habits. The team or organization takes advantage of synergy, where the sum of the parts is greater than the whole.

Once, a B State company brought me back to deal with a wonderful problem: "We're changing so fast we feel out of control."

After reviewing their efforts, I found they were still very much in command of all that was going on—they had merely experienced so much simultaneous progress they *felt* out of control. Their energy was so high and cohesive, they literally completed three to four times the number of projects and implemented ever-larger changes than when we first brought them out of silos and instituted cross-functional teamwork.

They had built up so much momentum and trust they no longer needed to check in with each other or stop their energy flow for so many meetings. Since they all accurately understood and represented each other's functional needs in the due course of their daily work, they could now operate more independently. They had the inertia of constant and continual forward movement.

They couldn't stop themselves.

At this Momentum stage, individuals and organizations are energized, positive, and excited. Results exceed expectations. People feel neither burned out nor overloaded—their elevated level of cooperation, communication, accountability, and support makes their job fun! This is the ultimate B State culture: high commitment, engagement, inspiration, and creativity. People enjoy a sense of invincibility—not as a state of perfection or ego, but as a desire to exceed previous levels of excellence. No problem is too great for the team to handle.

Return to A State? Inconceivable.

By now, in fact, any dyed-in-the-wool A State players have either gotten with the program or gone to a job in a more comfortable A State organization.

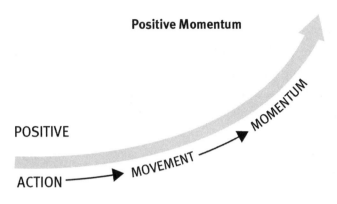

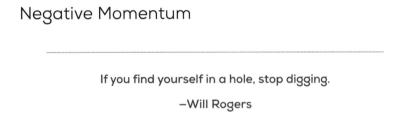

Figure 5: Building Positive Momentum

Negative Momentum

If you find yourself in a hole, stop digging.

–Will Rogers

No one is positive or negative all the time—our moods and energy ebb and flow in fluctuating waves similar to those of light and sound. We have minimal control over our natural waves, but we can choose where we place our attention. When we're in the ebb of a wave, we feel sluggish or a little down and might make "silly" mistakes—all natural manifestations of the bottom curve. We can't stop the ebb, but how we respond to it is entirely up to us. If we recognize we're having an off day or two, we can let it go, adapt to get through the situation, and know we'll naturally snap back in a little while.

Or we can get upset and take a negative **Stage One: Action.** We can look for excuses and blame the situation as unfair. We can—and often do—get irritated with everyone around us—our spouse, children, siblings, parents, teammates, or boss—for not living up to our standards, meeting our expectations, or supporting us enough.

All it takes to spark this negative flame and turn it into **Stage Two: Movement** is a thought we hardly notice. We dwell on a mistake, point fingers at others, or expend too much energy in regret or imagining others' criticism. With our energy and focus now split between our past mistake and our current project or task, we chastise ourselves. "Don't be stupid," I mutter to myself—but my wife thinks I'm talking to her. If my mood is bad enough, I might even bark at her for something incredibly inconsequential. Frustrations rise and conversations get louder and faster as we each throw evidence at the other to prove we're right.

We've now entered a *negative* **Stage Three: Momentum** that is as hard to stop as positive momentum. Energy ramps up even more when we try to get others to take our side, making it virtually impossible to solve problems or learn from experience. We're too invested in being right to entertain new ideas, new agreements, or even new peace overtures. Negative momentum builds mistrust, anger, and polarization that builds to ever-escalating conflict.

Negative Momentum

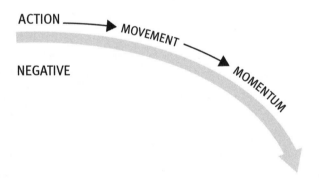

Figure 6: Building Negative Momentum

In the family, that means slammed doors, separations, and divorce. At the workplace, that means silo thinking, favoritism, and operational breakdowns. On the global stage, that translates to disenfranchisement, terrorism, bombs, and possibly even nuclear war.

Someone must take their foot off the gas pedal so the runaway "negative" car can glide to a stop—then everyone can take a breath and take the time to collect themselves or distract their attention from the trigger event. More often than not, that event was just a misunderstanding, too minor to justify all the inflammatory retaliations that followed.

Effectively Manage Energy

B State leaders learn to recognize these positive and negative energy cycles and how their actions or words can instigate or allow a negative movement/ momentum cycle to grow bigger.

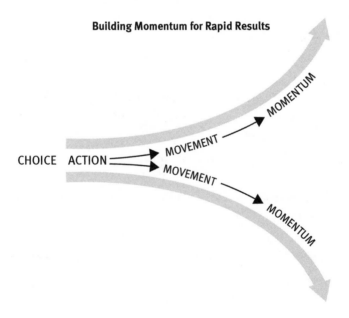

Figure 7: Building Momentum for Rapid Results: The Choice Is Yours

They also learn to foster a positive movement/momentum cycle by feeding it the appreciation, acknowledgment, and recognition that ramps it up even higher.

B State teams create clear agreements to surface and resolve difficult issues while maintaining everyone's safety. They commit to support and calm "triggered" people rather than confront them or perpetuate an us-versus-them stance. And they take immediate ownership for their own reactions so negative movement/momentum has no chance to build through the grapevine of opinion.

A divisional VP sent his team a confidential email before an upcoming company conference to present a rough draft of the differences between A State and B State leadership qualities they had been discussing. He asked for feedback or corrections. Some team members responded immediately with appreciation for the VP's clarification and offered suggestions to make the document feel less "judgmental." Others, however, took the A State description as personal criticism.

"I've worked at this company for over twenty years to make it successful!" one team member told his like-minded teammates. "How can he describe us like that?"

The offended created a *negative* **Stage Two: Movement** as they talked together and inflamed the group's emotional fire. Even though the document was a confidential rough draft, one manager shared it with his direct reports, which fanned the negative-momentum flames, spreading rumors, discomfort, and discontent down to the lower levels.

By the time I was contacted—a mere two weeks later—leaders were yelling at each other about their reactions to the "feedback desired" document and threatened to hand in their resignations. They were now in **Stage Three: Momentum**, where it was much harder to make an immediate shift without time to let the situation calm down.

After I coached the VP, he called for a leadership team meeting. He took ownership for his part in the misunderstanding, apologized for his "poor implementation," acknowledged those who'd sent their feedback, and explained why he sent out the document in the first place. "On the other hand," he continued, "I expect you to come to me directly when you have issues with my communications or messages. I don't appreciate you complaining or gossiping to each other or letting these kinds of misunderstandings fester. We must be more direct with each other, listen openly, and be willing to adjust our perspective if we're going to create a safe B State culture for ourselves and our employees. No one loses anything by the company transforming to a B State! Everyone wins."

The VP then met with each offended manager to personally reassure them of his intentions and offer his appreciation for their contribution to the organization's success. People calmed down and stopped fanning the negativity flames, but the team's trust had been broken. The negative momentum needed time to slow down. The VP learned that he needed to provide consistent reassuring feedback to help build back the trust. It took about two months before the leadership team returned to "normal."

Relationships at home work the same way. All it takes is one person—parent or child—to say something that someone else takes personally, and the same breakdown can occur. The key is to apologize and discuss a course correction as soon as possible so negative momentum has no chance to catch hold, but learning does. Otherwise, family members can end up not speaking to each other for weeks, months, years, or even decades.

True Innovation: *Receiving* versus *Thinking*

Knowledge speaks. Wisdom listens.

−Jimi Hendrix

Over time, I have learned to flip my "think of solutions" mode to a "quietly listen for an answer" mode when clients present difficult problems. A senior manager with a multinational organization once came to me with an unusual issue. He had developed a complex, three-dimensional process map and model to describe a new organizational structure and was so excited to share, he drew it on one of the whiteboards in a small conference room.

I honestly couldn't follow his drawing at all.

"I know what I want," he said, "I just can't figure out how to implement and make it work. What do you think I should do?"

"I'm not sure," I said, stalling. "Give me a moment."

I felt pressured, of course. *How am I going to come up with a way to implement something I don't understand? Crazy! I don't even know what questions to ask!*

I silently brainstormed ideas as I stared at the board, but I only got more confused and self-conscious. I was just about to admit, "You've stumped me," when I thought to look at the whiteboard on the other side of the room.

"I wonder: what's the best way to implement this new model?" I asked myself, staring at the blank board and waiting patiently for a solution to present itself.

And it did. I saw a picture in my mind of the first part of the implementation process. I looked back at his model to see whether the solution made sense. Sure enough, it did—and now I understood his model a little bit more.

I drew the steps I'd seen on the second whiteboard, then reflected on it and the original model. Suddenly, I saw the second implementation part, so I drew that as well. As each piece of the "puzzle" appeared to me, I understood his model better.

By the time I "saw" the third implementation phase, I fully understood his model. "Here's what you should do," I told him.

"Wow!" he exclaimed. "That'll work! And it makes me so mad! I consider myself super smart, but I've been thinking about this for three months and couldn't figure it out. You did in just a few minutes, and it's not only great, it's simple! How did you do it?"

I hoped that was a rhetorical question, because I certainly couldn't answer it. At that time, I still felt very insecure about my ability to "receive answers and solutions." Since I didn't think I was smart enough to come up with good answers on my own, I was grateful I could quiet myself without embarrassment to "listen" and "receive" them.

Now when one of my senior-consultant teammates notices my eyes looking "defocused and off to the side" during client meetings, they say, "Don't worry about Mark, he'll be back with you shortly—and with a very cool solution to your situation."

Our B State Culture Change and Mastership programs help executives and consultants develop their own ability to quickly diagnose complex organizational barriers and develop "inner listening" for inspired solutions. But while I learned to trust that process in client situations, for some reason it wasn't an instinctual reaction for my own business or personal problems. When I'm in solution-thinking mode and pressured to come up with the right answer, I generally feel restricted to previous solutions and stuck in worry, anxiety, and self-doubt about past failures. The negative energy builds until I feel completely paralyzed—like I used to feel whenever a teacher called me to the front of the class.

We generally do not come up with innovative answers and solutions when we're in a tight, restricted, pressured mental state or situation, such as a business meeting where it's not safe to give a "wrong" answer. We can't patiently wait for solutions to appear when we're multitasking with no clear sense of priority. Quiet reflection requires "space" to focus on what we desire. I'm all for brainstorming ideas in a group, but sometimes the best solutions come from sitting and listening for inner guidance.

8

External Drivers That Lead to Transformation

*Never change things by fighting the existing reality . . .
to change something, build a new model
that makes the existing model obsolete.*

—R. BUCKMINSTER FULLER

External drivers, or the circumstances we find ourselves in, shape our current reality—competition, customer demands, economic conditions, government regulations, technological advancements . . . the list is endless. The common element in all external drivers is our lack of control. No matter how we vote, for example, we cannot personally impact the country's economy. If our organization does not rise to meet the challenge when an entrepreneur springs up with a new technique, or product, or service, it may end up out of business.

That's what happened when Eastman Kodak's leadership ignored the challenge of digital technology. After more than one hundred years as the undisputed king of all things photography, Kodak's products became obsolete within a single decade, and the company had to completely refigure its operations. But since that effort was so late, they're no longer anywhere near the top of their industry.

It Happens to Us All

External drivers impact us personally, as well. I had been preparing for a 20 percent growth in my business when the 2008 economic downturn hit, and I ended up suffering a 75 percent loss instead. I not only had to make huge reductions in my operating expenses, but had to decide how much of my own money I was willing to invest to keep my business afloat.

That was a stressful, depressing time in my life. The economic crash—an external driver—hadn't been my fault. I didn't play the stock market and I didn't flip properties. But I had invested a lot of money and effort during the previous twenty-five-plus years to build my practice. Just when business seemed to have turned a corner—with steady growth and three years of financial gains under my belt—I faced losing everything in bankruptcy. Like millions of others, I felt as if everything was out of my control. I was a victim.

That's how external drivers work. A sudden illness, a death in the family, a layoff, a natural disaster—even an unexpected relationship breakup—will always throw us for a loop, no matter how prepared we think we are.

My fear increased every day as I looked at my bills and knew I didn't have enough income to pay them. I maxed out my credit cards, then emptied my retirement and personal savings. With each new loss, I felt more hopeless and depressed. My personal value had always been based on my ability to provide good service to clients, who were now minimal, and support my family, whose financial security I was now depleting. At my lowest point, I realized I was worth more dead than alive—if I kept up my life-insurance policy payments. I was in a very scary and self-destructive place.

But I was an expert in accountability and had successfully designed the Personal Accountability Model in the mid-eighties, which I described in *Making Yourself Indispensable: The Power of Personal Accountability*. I knew I needed to get clear with my intention and purpose to transform my situation. I also knew my purpose needed to be larger than "get out of my current situation." I had to stop obsessing over my financial problems and change my focus to something that would get me moving in a positive direction.

I created a new purpose for myself: support and serve others. That inspired me to review my unique talents and abilities, including the natural skills I was born with and had developed over the years. I realized external drivers might take away my clients, business, and money, but nothing could take away those talents and abilities: consulting and coaching skills and the ability to teach math. I decided to consult for a nonprofit organization, coach an individual who'd been promoted to plant manager, and tutor a friend's eleven-year-old son, who was failing math, among other subjects.

I helped all three for free—just to get me out of the house so I'd stop thinking about my financial problems and bankruptcy fears.

Within three or four weeks, my positive energy was back. It was the first time I ever valued having a clear purpose that not only reflected my contribution to something greater than myself, but used my unique, God-given talents to achieve it. I didn't make any more money than before, but I developed a high sense of confidence and self-esteem, higher than at any other time in my life. In fact, I felt better about myself at that point than I felt even when my business and previous books were so successful.

The nonprofit organization got through its difficult period and returned to business as usual. The plant manager became highly successful. But my greatest sense of gratitude came from young Josh's success.

His counselors had recommended he be moved to an "alternative school," where he wouldn't be so challenged. I told his parents, "Before you make that decision, let me tutor him in math to figure out what's really going on."

The first thing I did was *not* assume Josh was poor at math, even though all the "measurable evidence" indicated he was. Measurements too often don't tell the complete story or expose the root causes of a problem. In fact, sometimes they're so misleading they generate bad assumptions or wrong conclusions.

I looked at Josh's last failed test and asked him to point out the section in his math book that covered the kind of problems he'd gotten wrong. "You know what?" I said. "I haven't done these kinds of problems for at least thirty years. Can you show me how to do them?"

When he just gave me a strange look, I said, "If you could just walk me through one of these problems and show me how to do it, I'm sure I'll remember."

In front of my eyes, Josh went from slouching and distracted to sitting up and being direct with me. Pointing to a problem, he broke it down into steps, each of which he explained very clearly. He understood perfectly how to do the problems on the test he had failed.

"Okay, it's coming back to me now," I said, "but can you do a few problems from the book, so I can see you do it?"

He solved the first problem perfectly. He made an arithmetic error in the second problem and so got it wrong. He made even more calculation mistakes in the third problem—and began getting distracted and impatient. Finally, he threw down his pencil in complete frustration. "I told you I can't do math! It's impossible for me to learn or understand it!"

Clearly, Josh's beliefs didn't match reality, but his low grades and teachers' conclusions had reinforced them enough to "prove" his irrational self-image. But the root cause of Josh's math dysfunction had nothing to do with a lack of intelligence or mathematic competency. The reality, in fact, was exactly the opposite—he didn't have the patience to solve what were, for him, overly simple problems. I had to disprove his beliefs and respond to his "distractive" tendencies. In other words, I had to slow him down enough to check his work so his impatience to "just get it over with" did not hinder his ability to achieve good grades.

I taught him how to interrupt his own distractions and stay focused, even when the work was "boring." Then I taught him quick ways to check his work.

Josh's grades began to improve immediately, but he did not change his personal belief that he "couldn't do math" until the end of the year, when he earned an A in math and improved in all his other subjects. He proved he could believe in himself.

By the end of the second year, he was a straight-A student. Within another two years he was moved to a top private school in Los Angeles's GATE (Gifted and Talented Education) program. He maintained his straight-A average through Advanced Placement classes in high school, and eventually got accepted at one of his top-choice universities.

What Did I Learn?

Mastery—the speed with which you recognize
what is unfolding in front of you, and the capacity to act
appropriately to create the best outcome.

—Michael Nila, founder, Blue Courage

Working with Josh gave me quite an education. I learned to not make assumptions or judgments about people, no matter how things appear. I gave Josh the benefit of the doubt. I looked for the truth underneath his behavior. I did not use "measurement" or "metrics" as an absolute indicator of the truth.

I took that realization with me when I went back to leading my consulting business. I viewed my consultants differently. I looked for *their* unique talents and abilities and found ways to better utilize them not only within the organization, but with our clients. I asked for their advice more often. I recommended they work with different clients based on their individual abilities.

I matched one person's strength with another's weakness and had them coach each other. I stopped micromanaging to make them conform to my consulting style. I accepted they each had their own manner, personality, and approach different from mine—and that was okay. In fact, it was usually better for our clients.

Now, when someone doesn't perform well or keep a commitment, I don't assume the worst. I ask questions to better understand them and the situation rather than jump to conclusions and, as a result, now have a better relationship with all my people—and they've noticed. They say I'm not as reactive as I used to be. I don't play the "blame game" the way I used to. I'm much more open to ideas and far more flexible about making changes.

Best of all, I feel better about my communications with them and how I run my organization. Since I let go of my need to control and got more relaxed with my business, it's doing much better, and I feel a sense of peace about how I make my living.

9

Create Your New Reality—
The Key Step for Transformation

The best way to predict the future is to create it.

−PETER DRUCKER

If not for the 2008 economic downturn, I wouldn't have had the time to help Josh. Sometimes, external drivers act as wake-up calls to make changes we've been avoiding, or to spur creative solutions that raise our standards of behavior, performance, service, or success.

Sometimes, that wake-up call comes from our own success.

Great Leaders Create Pictures of Success

Figure 8: B State Implementation Model

Changemaking happens when people fall in love
with a different version of the future.

—Seth Godin

Steve Jobs's vision for Apple changed our lives forever. Frank Dulcich, CEO of Pacific Seafood Group, reinvented his company from a single Portland retail store to a $1.5 billion multinational organization. They and all other great CEOs start with a vision of something that never existed before and share the kind of imagination it takes to create a new future reality. But to be successful, as all innovative CEOs discover, a company must mature from its entrepreneurial beginnings, where people rally around and are influenced by their vision, to an organization with multiple leadership levels, in which people are more influenced by their direct manager or supervisor—even though it's still the visionary CEO's company.

Once that tiered organization becomes established, its thinking, behaviors, and communications also solidify—in fact, they become "embedded habits" that inadvertently lock the organization into its current level of success (or failure). To grow beyond that success—or even just maintain it in the face of increased competition, market changes, and fluctuating economies—the company must constantly reinvent itself, because the CEO's vision is no longer enough to inspire change.

At that point, leadership needs to create a meaningful Picture of Success and Purpose Statement, but they're typically locked into old mind-sets and habits meant only to ensure their own individual success. They bring in great programs like Lean and Six Sigma to install "continuous improvement systems," "training workshops," and "team-building retreats," but all those primarily *improve upon the past and current reality*, rather than create new futures. They don't prepare leaders for the creative thinking they need to reinvent their organization.

And that's how many very successful corporations go into decline—or even go out of business.

Remember Tom from chapter 1, the Milstun Corporation CIO with a clear vision to centralize his organization? His team members were too stuck in their silo-and-divisional control paradigm to follow his lead. He needed an outside consultant to unlock them from their embedded thinking, so they could create a new Picture of Success to guide their centralization efforts.

So did Brian, CEO of Braston Medical Center (BMC), a hospital located two and a half hours from the nearest airport that served a community largely made up of Medicare patients. With reimbursement coming primarily from the government (the ultimate slow—and low—payer) rather than from insurance companies or private-pay individuals, they could not leverage the costs of all their various specialties across multiple hospitals the way larger health-care corporations typically do.

Caught between rising costs and declining reimbursement, BMC constantly struggled to keep its doors open. Even major initiatives to cut costs and develop new revenue streams could not bring them out of the red. The last thing they wanted was to sell out to a larger corporation, which would reduce their hospital to a satellite facility that only offered basic care and would force community members to travel great distances for cancer, heart disease, diabetes, and other specialized treatments.

After putting in so much effort yet still falling short of revenue goals, the senior leadership team (SLT) was frustrated and exhausted—as were their employees. Staff hadn't received any bonuses or even cost-of-living increases for two of the preceding three years. Most caregivers were still dedicated to their patients and provided good care, but morale was low, turnover high, and performance metrics only came to "average"—never "exceptional" or even "good." And that, of course, resulted in financial penalties, which lowered their reimbursements even further.

The energy in the room felt hopeless and despairing the first day I met the senior leadership team and let them spend a couple of hours describing their circumstances. They clearly did not know how to change their situation.

"You *must* choose," I finally announced. "Do you want to sell out to a larger health-care corporation, or are you committed to do whatever it takes to keep this organization alive? You must choose—and your choice at this stage must be nonnegotiable. If you decide to keep your organization afloat, as it seems you all really want, I'll give you a clear B State road map. But you must give me your immutable, one-hundred-percent commitment."

"But we've been trying to keep the doors open, and we're barely making it!" one team member said. "We're not sure it's even possible to get us back in the black. The hospital may have run its course."

I knew a B State transformation was the organization's best shot to stay alive, but the team needed a clear commitment—they couldn't be on the fence about selling or not selling. They had to draw a line in the sand and not straddle it.

"I recognize all your efforts," I said, "and I applaud you for getting this far, but you're right: what you've been doing won't be good enough for the future. You need to transform to survive. So, let me ask you this: Just how important is it to the community to stay in business? Are you willing to do whatever it takes to not close and not sell? In other words, are you in, or are you out?"

I waited as they looked at each other. Finally, one of the more senior team members stood up. "I am completely committed to keeping our doors open in service to our community. We're too important to them for us to close. I also want to be confident that we've given our full one hundred percent to that outcome, so I can live with the results regardless of what happens."

"Yes!"

"Me too."

With that simple rallying point, the team came back to life and agreed, individually and as a unit, to implement my B State transformation program.

Picture Success

BMC's mission statement was mundane, common, and uninspiring: "To provide excellent care to every patient, every time." Their vision statement was equally lackluster: "To be the regional medical center of excellence." Neither provided a clear sense of purpose, despite meeting the common criteria to "focus on the desired result" and "sound good enough" for a website and marketing materials. We needed to develop the SLT's dedication to survival into a B State Picture of Success that spoke to the mind-set, attitudes, and behaviors necessary to achieve and sustain their desired result.

We couldn't create a single picture for the entire organization—no one could be accountable for that. We had to create it *specifically* for the SLT— the ones who would lead the hospital's survival—and only look for those mind-sets, attitudes, and behaviors they would do *differently* to ensure that survival. There was no point picturing what they were already doing—that's what got them into their current predicament!

Don't put a limit on anything.
The more you dream, the further you get.

–Michael Phelps

I asked each SLT member to answer three questions within five minutes, following three rules:

1. All answers had to be a "stretch" and offer "do differ-ently" mind-sets, attitudes, and behaviors, not things they currently did well and wanted to continue.

2. No clichés or slogans. No "world class" or "better than the best" nonsense. Only behavior, attitude, and mind-set descriptions that were different from their current state.

3. Answer as if it's a year from now.

Question #1: What is your *new reputation* as senior leaders and as a senior leadership team now that you've successfully led the dramatic change that saved the medical center?

· What did you do differently that set clear direction and expectations?

- How did you communicate differently to demonstrate your unified team's alignment, unity, and focus?
- What kind of risks did you take to improve organizational effectiveness and efficiency?
- How did you engage your employees differently?
- And how do you hold them accountable now?

Question #2: How does your team operate now to support your new reputation?

- What's different about how you share information with each other?
- What's different about how you hold each other accountable?
- How do you now responsively surface and solve problems as a team?
- What makes your current conflict resolution and decision-making more timely and inclusive?

Question #3: How did the organization, its employees, and the community benefit from your new SLT behavior?

- How did you ensure the organization's profitability?
- How did you effectively respond to the community's needs?
- How did you effectively engage and hold physicians accountable while ensuring patient satisfaction?

I collected everyone's answers one question at a time and recorded them all on flip charts. Then I split them into three groups—one for each question—and had each one write a paragraph describing the boldest, most different behaviors recorded, using these four rules:

1. No slogans or brief explanations—nothing easy to memorize and recite. Describe the "different" attitudes, behaviors, and mind-sets as completely as possible.

2. No bullet points. Write a full paragraph that tells a story rather than a criteria list or set of disjointed goals.

3. No political correctness. Nothing will be shared or submitted for anyone else's opinion or approval, so be as bold and unconventional and even outlandish as you want to be.

4. You'll be tested, so if what you write isn't significantly different from your current mind-set, attitude, and behavior, you'll have to rewrite it!

I gave them half an hour. Most took forty-five minutes. Then I had each group apply the test:

> Rate your current performance against your paragraph on a 1–5 scale where 5 = we currently operate exactly as we described in the paragraph and 1 = we don't operate at all like we described in the paragraph.

If the individual scores averaged higher than 2.25, they had to rewrite—their paragraph didn't describe a big- or bold-enough change.

A couple of groups struggled to "stretch" enough in their initial paragraph. They had no problem writing something that sounded good and motivational—I even liked what they wrote—but it wasn't detailed enough to pass the test. Needless to say, they were shaken. Normally, their work would have been done. Instead, they had to dig deeper to clearly articulate what they would specifically—not generally—be doing differently a year from now.

"You don't have to rewrite completely," I told them. "Remove or modify any remarks that rate a 3.5 or 4 to demonstrate how those specific elements will be different from what you're doing now."

After rewriting to pass the test, their behavior descriptions were clearer, punchier, stronger—and more inspiring! Plus, they better understood what they'd be accountable for, and learned that while hype and clichés do not inspire people, *clarity* builds the confidence that leads to inspiration.

Each group presented their paragraph to the rest of the team so they could ask questions, challenge statements, and make modifications as a group. Once all the paragraphs were fully edited—which, in this case, took about thirty minutes—I read them aloud as a whole so the entire team could see how they flowed together.

> The senior leadership team (SLT) sets, communicates, and demonstrates clear direction for the medical center. The direction is determined by honest examination of external drivers. We operate with a consistent purpose. The SLT provides the resources our employees and physicians need to achieve our chosen purpose. We provide a culture that promotes trust to take action to achieve our purpose. We provide encouragement and specific guidance to remove obstacles to achieving our purpose. We recognize improved and effective execution. By focusing on and tracking our purpose, we recognize the need for recovery.
>
> The SLT utilizes our collective skills to achieve organizational goals. We are open, honest, and responsive with direct reports, physicians, and ourselves. We follow through in a timely manner on both small and large issues. We communicate openly to facilitate change and enhance mutual trust, respect, and accountability to ensure decisions are based on organizational needs. We resolve conflicts through quick identification and open discussion in a respectful and forgiving atmosphere.
>
> We provide a clear purpose in response to external forces resulting in the long-term viability of

our medical center as an independent freestanding community-driven health system. We promote a culture that attracts and retains high performers. The environment we provide supports quick course changes and resilience in the workforce.

"Wow!" someone said. "The flow between each paragraph is amazing! It's as if *one person* wrote all three!"

"That's because you are all at the same consciousness level," I said. "You're all at the top of the triangle."

B State Consciousness Triangle

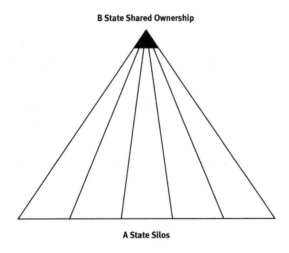

Figure 9: The B State Consciousness Triangle

You must learn a new way to think
before you can master a new way to be.

—Marianne Williamson

In the triangle pictured in figure 9, the bottom represents those functional areas that generally operate in silos and thus focus only on their own optimization. Since they all have different priorities, constraints, metrics, and even language, trying to work together raises almost unavoidable conflict, which typically results in unsolvable lose-lose compromises or win-lose power plays.

Someone outside the conflict and midway up the triangle, such as human resources or a consultant or an upper manager, can use their broader perspective to provide solutions those at the bottom cannot see. But we only think about what's best for the organization as a whole when we're at the top of the triangle, where differences between functional areas disappear.

That's where our customers are—when they receive damaged goods, they don't say, "Gee, I wonder which department messed this up!" They say, "Damn, I should have bought a different brand!"—so that's where the B State is.

"Shared ownership," that oft-bandied term, doesn't mean everyone must be involved in every decision, or that we won't run into new conflicts as we try to resolve old ones. It means we're all invested in eliminating anything obstructing the organization's success, whether or not we're directly involved in those obstructions. "It's not my problem" and "It's not my job" don't exist at the top of the triangle. "It" *is* their problem—and everyone else's problem on the team and in the organization.

How is it *not* the whole team's problem if an infielder keeps missing grounders? How can a band not "take ownership" to fix the issue if a backup singer consistently flubs a particular harmony? Authors and consultants who talk about putting the organization first generally offer advice that flows from the bottom up: "Here's what my area—my group, my team, my results—can do to benefit the company's overall success." But that's classic stuck-in-a-silo A State thinking.

A senior VP of marketing took his leadership team—two directors and a midlevel VP he'd been mentoring for more than three years—to lunch. On the way to the restaurant, the midlevel VP suggested a process change that would support another department's revenue stream. "We're not here to support any other department's revenue!" the senior VP exploded. "I don't get a bonus for their business! That's it—we're done! I'm not going to keep mentoring anyone so disloyal!"

He was *really* stuck in the A State—and, frankly, disloyal to his organization. It's a common scenario: a department significantly reduces its operating costs by hundreds of thousands every month by streamlining its processes, yet in doing so negatively impacts five other departments, which raises the organization's costs by millions. At the bottom of the triangle, that first department celebrates its major success—but at the top, it's now a liability.

Fortunately, the entire BMC SLT's consciousness was so aligned that their output was *also* aligned, even though their paragraphs addressed different topics.

Your Personal Success

You, too, may need a B State transformation to create the new reality you desire. Creating a Picture of Success of your new future reality is not about developing goals, metrics, or priorities. It's about imagining the ideal behaviors, feelings, and thoughts you'd like to embody today and from now on.

My personal Picture of Success was about living with my ideal life partner. Yours might be about reinventing your life.

Maybe you want your spouse, children, or parental relationships to transform so you can enjoy more openness, trust, and intimacy.

Maybe you want to transform your health but are tired of diets and gym memberships you don't use.

Maybe you want to renovate your career, which has plateaued despite all the personal coaches, certificate courses, and "prosperity" guidance you've gone through.

If you just feel stuck and aren't sure why—whatever the cause—it's time to revitalize your nonnegotiable Picture of Success. A Picture of Success doesn't provide a makeover road map, but the act of creating it will mentally, emotionally, and physically prepare you to manifest expansion. This is not "just another goal." It's a transformation: a new way of thinking, an evolved set of the feelings and actions you will experience in your new reality.

I first learned the value of this during the opening game of a National Basketball Association championship series when the sportscaster interviewed Isaiah Thomas, who was starting for the Boston Celtics for the first time.

"Isaiah, you are one of the youngest ballplayers to be in the NBA championship series. Are you nervous?"

Isaiah tilted his head. "Not at all! I've pictured myself defending, shooting baskets, and running up and down the court in this championship series a thousand times since I was seven years old. This game isn't new for me. In fact, I finally feel at home being here to play it."

As an Author . . .

You did not come to face reality.
You came to create reality.

—Abraham-Hicks

When I sat down to write this book, I remembered how long and how much I'd struggled to write my four previous titles. The more I pored over those experiences, the more I put off getting started on this one. A full year passed before I put pen to paper—actually, fingers to keyboard—when I faced a second common challenge: I needed to do it right!

"Being right" and "doing it right" were great stalling devices, so whenever anyone asked about my progress, I made up a story. "I'm going through a 'birthing' process," I'd say. "It's difficult and time consuming, but I'm working on it. Honest."

I knew I could picture a more positive approach to the work, but I didn't have the courage to seek a new option for the longest time. I let myself be a "victim" of my past by concluding my previous struggles would dictate my future authorship. We all do it: use our negative past as a reference point for our future. Rehash mistakes so repetitively they still generate the same heat, disappointment, and discouragement that coursed through us then, even though the incident took place years ago. Then repeat the same experience— or, as happens so often, "learn from our mistakes," that most common reason organizations change so slowly.

Learning from our mistakes may advance us to a *better* A State, but we're still stuck in A State, still bringing in consultants to assess our organization, holding training workshops, and buying process-improvement programs. We forever push onward to yet another, minimally better A State rather than *boldly* respond to the constantly changing demands of business.

I didn't want to repeat the past or just learn from it. Besides, I could not imagine how long it would take me to become a better writer. Probably years. Possibly forever.

My only choice was to create a B State transformation and imagine a *different* future—a *different* way of doing what I had already done four times too slowly, painfully, and frustratingly.

So, I wrote a personal Picture of Success.

Picture of Success for Writing My Book

I am having a fantastic time writing my newest and most important book to date. This book represents all my concepts, strategies, and tools for achieving breakthrough results with a new paradigm I call the B State.

My experience writing this book is fun, insightful, and inspiring. I am very open about putting forth my most bold ideas without censorship for ensuring others will like it. I am also using an "inner-outer" approach to writing, where I center myself, connect with my inner guidance, and listen for direction rather than write from an outline.

I enjoy the process of rereading my book as I write it without criticizing myself—instead, I'm learning how to fine-tune, change, and rewrite it without being pressured by time, frustration, or a need for perfection. In fact, I just see the entire process as a natural form of getting out my ideas and learning to articulate them more clearly.

I am using outside experts or coaches to guide me. I am finding the perfect person who gets my vision, understands my desired outcome, and doesn't judge me for my current level of writing. In fact, he or she inspires and stretches me to be even better and teach me along the way. Our relationship is fun, as we work well together and laugh a lot.

Instead of giving up my power in that relationship due to their expertise, I speak up when something is missing, or when I don't like a section and want to rewrite what the "expert" has written. I stay very dedicated to the integrity of my message and the inspiration I receive along the way.

With my book complete, I feel I gave it my very best and am proud of it, regardless of how it sells or reads to others. This book was born out of love, commitment, and fun.

I inserted this Picture of Success and am writing these words in the seventh month of actively working on the book you are reading. I hired a writing coach who perfectly matches the description above. I'm having a blast and learning tons. My wife says she's never seen me so enthusiastic and happy during any writing project. I've learned to speak up more and stay true to my voice and message rather than give up my authority to an expert, as I've done so many times in the past.

10

The Purpose Statement

A hero is someone who has given his or her life
to something bigger than oneself.
–JOSEPH CAMPBELL

Once the BMC senior leadership team completed their Picture of Success, they developed a Purpose Statement:

> To preserve our Medical Center as a comprehensive, independent, community-driven health system to optimize access to quality health care for patients in the communities we serve.

The team acted differently from that point on. They looked at their old problems in new ways. They worked together with greater unity and made decisions faster than ever before. And they were so inspired by their new sense of purpose, they planned to share it with their middle managers.

"Survival is nonnegotiable," they said. "We expect everyone to be committed to this cause."

The Power of Our Minds to Serve or Defeat

Our amazing, powerful minds automatically produce action-packed movies—in living color with complete surround sound—that put a negative or positive spin on our past, present, and future. We cannot stop these memories and dreams from playing out in our heads. They're part of the human experience. But we can, we *must*, learn to direct their positive and negative aspects, or we will continue to create our future based on our past—rather than on our imagining it.

The past will always contain aspects of what didn't work, but the future can be created from a clean slate, free of breakdowns. We must use our minds and imagination to serve us rather than lead us backward to all the fear, blame, disappointment, hurt, defeat, anger, and, in extreme cases, violence we previously experienced.

We must *embody* our goals, not just aim to achieve them. Whatever we achieve, we can *un-achieve*. How often have you fixed a problem only to have it circle back again later? Achieving any goal involves willpower, but when willpower tires, we naturally revert to old patterns—our mental and emotional selves are still stuck in A State despite our physical efforts to push them out.

When we *embody* our goals instead—when we let go of the past and create a clear Picture of Success as a focal point for all change efforts—we physically, mentally, and emotionally move into B State. We become a "new person" who naturally sustains our embodied changes—which is why they can happen so swiftly.

Defeat Turns into Success

I have learned over the years that
when one's mind is made up, this diminishes fear;
knowing what must be done does away with fear.

—Rosa Parks

BMC's SLT committed to begin every meeting by reading their Purpose Statement as a reference point to solve problems and make decisions. It gave everyone permission—and safety—to surface problems they previously hid. The middle managers soon did the same thing. With everyone clearly focused on survival, "safe" engagement extended down to the lowest employee levels. The entire organization's "vibration" increased as people became more innovative and took more initiative and greater ownership for their role in the medical center's survival. It theoretically takes two years or longer to change an organization's culture, but this B State transformation significantly changed people's mind-sets and behaviors in a single day. Their habits didn't solidify that fast, of course, but their initial adjustment was so substantial, we could measure the culture change in only six months.

SHORT-TERM PURPOSES

BMC's mission-statement purpose may have been to provide quality medical service to the community, but their short-term purpose was simply survival—a clear rallying focus everyone could support. Once they were stable, their short-term purpose would change back to "growth" so as to better serve their community.

Other organizational short-term purposes might be as follows:

- Build a foundation to support future growth.
- Expand into new global markets.
- Become lean and eliminate waste.
- Provide the highest level of customer experience.
- Develop leaders at every level.

Problem-solving, decision-making, and time/energy focus demand a clear purpose that helps set priorities, leverage resources, and stay on the "straight and narrow" when emotional wants and desires arise to distract you. When my business faced bankruptcy, my short-term purpose was to get out of debt. I initially put myself on a strict allowance of $1,000 per month and used all other funds to pay down my high-interest credit cards. It was hard, but my clear purpose kept me on track to eliminate over $750,000 worth of business and personal debt in forty-two months. Once I fulfilled my short-term purpose, I could start building again.

THE MYTH OF "FINDING YOUR PURPOSE"

Too many of us are not living our dreams
because we are living our fears.

–Les Brown

Young adults and the coaching industry are obsessed with "discovering your purpose," but essential as that may be, "purpose" is not a one-time thing. Our life's purpose changes as we evolve and circumstances change. So do our unique gifts and abilities—they're not static either. I was a winning baseball pitcher in high school, for example, with my sights set on going pro. I was so dedicated—my life purpose was so clear and compelling—I worked hard both on- and off-season to prepare.

But then a professional ballplayer told me, "Mark, I clocked you. You'll never make it in the pros. Your fastball just isn't fast enough—you'll never get out of the minors."

I was only eighteen, so I reconciled to find another life purpose and play just for fun in summer leagues and men's softball. But my original goal hadn't been a waste of time. I not only learned dedication—I learned about teamwork and leadership and healthy competition. Plus, I developed a unique skill I've cherished my entire life.

In my early twenties, I took on a new life purpose to make use of another natural gift: my ability to teach high school math. My students advanced quickly, but I just as quickly realized that it wasn't the right fit for me.

Sometimes we change our purpose due to ability limitations. Other times, we just outgrow it, like an old set of clothes—or a first romance. But sometimes, it changes naturally as we move beyond our own limiting beliefs. I never intended or dreamed I would create my own methodology, much less write books, when I began my consulting business. But as my career evolved, I rose above my limiting self-image to develop a greater purpose than anything I had ever dreamed possible.

Unfortunately, many young adults believe they must wait to "find" their purpose before they invest themselves in a job or career. Some who aren't clear about their purpose don't even try to get a job because they mistakenly believe they can't get work until they know who they are. Others get jobs but quit within months—they either don't believe the work is aligned with their purpose, or they don't get promoted fast enough to match their "ideal" time frame based on their self-anointed sense of expertise. In an instant-gratification world that drives expectations—both our own and those we perceive coming from others—it's hard to be patient. But only those who are patient can enjoy the *process* of growth and development.

Truth be told, whatever purpose we have today is temporary and evolutionary. If we invest in our current job or career, it will evolve to take us in new directions, to new goals, or even to unexpected careers. Sometimes, just having a job is a purpose in itself—it provides a sense of self-worth, a pathway to new skills and knowledge, and, of course, the means for independent living.

Drummer, ballplayer, high school teacher, consultant, leadership innovator, author—my purpose continues to change as my skills and knowledge grow and my interests evolve. And I'm not done yet. I don't know what my purpose will be in my later years. Where others look forward to retirement, I see myself evolving yet again to master new and exciting challenges.

11

B State Priorities
and Shared Ownership

The secret of change is to focus all your energy
not on fighting the old, but on building the new.

—DAN MILLMAN

Braston Medical Center's SLT had completed their organizational strategic-planning process a month before I started working with them, establishing annual priorities based on the six key pillars or "big rocks" of their business: customer satisfaction, quality, financial health, business growth, culture, and safety. Their middle managers, though, still complained they had no clear direction.

Figure 10: B State Implementation Model

"We still have more priority projects than we have resources to accomplish them."

"New priorities keep getting added without any old ones taken off."

"I try to navigate between competing priorities, but when I select the one I think is more important, I get blamed for not making enough progress on the other!"

In light of this disconnect, I asked each senior manager to individually write down the organization's top five to seven priorities—not their department's priorities, the organization's.

"If I think of an eighth priority," one person asked, "can I add it?"

"Sure—but focus on the ones you feel are most important."

They were done in about five minutes.

"Now, one at a time, give me a priority from your list for the flip chart so we can review them all together. If someone shares one of yours, cross it off your page so we don't duplicate answers. I'll keep going around the room until everyone has exhausted their list. When yours is empty, just say 'pass.'"

By the end of the process, they had identified *thirty-one* different top organizational priorities—thirty-one! This was the group that believed their strategic plan was "clear."

"That's okay," I assured them. "Most senior leadership teams identify between twenty-five and forty different priorities—and that's down from ten years ago, when the average number was between thirty-five and sixty! But ask yourself: Do you think your *thirty-one different priorities* provide a clear sense of direction to anyone? Do you think you can effectively monitor all those priorities at the same time? Do you understand why your middle managers are confused? I'm confused!"

Routine, Improvement, and B State Priorities

"Priority" clearly means "This is more important than everything else." Stop the bleeding, *then* clean up the floor. But different kinds of priorities often cause confusion about what is *most* important. Routine priorities, for example, are the daily activities that keep the business operational—and there are hundreds of them. They're not optional—they're essential tasks: take a patient's vitals, fit two production parts together, complete supervisory schedules, lead project meetings. We normally don't consider them priorities until we're short staffed, lack resources, or have an operational crisis. Then they suddenly "take priority" and become the most important items on our plate.

When routine tasks become ineffective or inefficient, they're taken up as cross-functional or single-department "improvement" projects. If the flow between purchasing and accounting breaks down, for example, management may launch a "Lean" process-improvement project or create new policies and procedures to improve operational safety. If HR gets a lot of complaints, it may institute training programs to elevate employees' "people skills." Yet, while several improvement projects may take place at the same time—and while they're critical for elevating an organization from A to A+ State—they should never take precedence over daily customer-satisfaction priorities.

When you lead one of those continuous-improvement projects, you "own" it and are accountable for its success, so you naturally rank it right after your essential "routine" priorities. As a result, you might not have the wherewithal to support *other* "owners" leading *other* improvement projects— and they might not have the time or willingness to support *yours*. Hence, priorities conflict and new silos arise, even if both projects are cross-functional.

B State projects are transformational "game changers," not just "continuous improvement" efforts. They significantly impact business results and so require a cultural adjustment. They might replace old equipment with newer versions that modify employees' roles and expectations, or scrap manual systems for automation. B State business models may attract new markets, accommodate acquisitions and mergers, or undertake significant role changes, such as converting a sales organization from transactional to strategic.

Some consultants claim a company can only strive for one or two such "game-changing" goals per year, but I've seen organizations achieve six to eight B State projects while still maintaining their routine and continuous-improvement priorities.

Senior leadership chooses its B State transformational projects based on their Picture of Success and external drivers. While every venture, large or small, requires a leader, B State project leaders don't individually *own* them as they would in A State circumstances. Instead, the entire senior leadership team takes ownership and accountability for their success. That doesn't mean the project is run by consensus—not every team member is involved with every decision—but every team member is *accountable* for resolving any disruptions that cannot be handled by the "steering committee" or project team. Most important, everyone in the organization is aware of and responsible for directly or indirectly supporting those six to eight "nonnegotiable" B State transformation projects. In fact, regular general-progress updates are shared with all employees, so everyone has a clear sense of direction, focus, and priority.

Shared Ownership for B State Priority Projects

Alone we can do so little;
together we can do so much.

—Helen Keller

When I finished explaining the differences between types of priorities, several of the BMC senior leadership team members nodded, but others wanted to know more about how it worked. I said, "Let's get clear on *your* B State priority projects first, and then use them to illustrate how it works. Write down your top five of the thirty-one priorities on the walls around this room in order of preference—first choice, second choice, third choice, and so on—using these two criteria:

1. Which projects are most critical for transforming from A State to B State based on your Picture of Success?

2. Which are the most cross-functional? (i.e., Which ones impact and involve the largest cross section of your organization?)

Almost everyone selected the same two projects as important. I called those "primary priorities." Another four received votes from at least half the team, making them "secondary priorities." Three received a moderate number of votes, so I listed them on a separate page. The rest of the projects each received one or no votes.

"Will completing your primary and secondary priorities move you toward accomplishing your Picture of Success?"

"Yes," they all agreed.

"It'd be amazing to focus on those six and make sure they happen," one person said.

"But it's critical to also include one of the priorities listed in the third section," another put in. "Based on the eventual impact of that project next year, I really think it should be included now."

The others agreed.

"So, we're agreed on two primary and five secondary nonnegotiable organizational priorities," I summarized. "Does that mean no one will address the other twenty-four issues you listed as priorities?"

"No," someone answered. "Those will stay on our departmental lists of continuous-improvement projects. They just won't have the entire team's focus."

Since all seven projects were already in progress, it wasn't hard to identify which team member led each one. "Do you have a written project plan," I asked, "that clearly documents your intended outcome with completion milestones and due dates?"

Five did, two didn't—including one who claimed their project was already 30 percent complete. I shook my head. "How do you know it's thirty percent if you don't have a plan of what you're completing?"

Everyone laughed.

"Don't be so fast to mock," I warned. "Let me ask you five who do have plans: Have any other team members reviewed it?"

Only one person raised a hand.

"Yup," I said. "That's what happens about 95 percent of the time—and it's how teams end up back in silos. How can you problem-solve or 'share ownership' for every priority project's success if you don't know its desired outcomes, strategies, or expected challenges? You can't—you'd be working completely in the dark, not understanding enough about the plan to provide good critical-thinking input. Naturally, you'd have no ownership. Naturally, you'd tune out when anything other than your own project was discussed."

"Yeah," one person said sheepishly. "That's just what happens at every meeting!"

"Let's be real," I said. "You cannot *all* be intricately involved in *all* projects. But you *can* be for the top seven we just identified, so make a commitment: you will each complete your project's plan or charter and share it with all teammates before your next meeting in two weeks. Any objections?"

There were no objections.

Shared Ownership in Action

"Now," I went on, "before you react to what I am going to say next, take a deep breath and prepare to hear me out. Ready? Good—because I want to talk about one of the biggest problems leadership teams face. You all know it: a project leader shows up at a meeting and announces they've made an autonomous decision to push back their milestone target dates by several weeks. It puts the project at risk and effectively cuts out their teammates' ownership, but since no one realizes that's what just happened—and they all want to be supportive—everyone says, 'Okay, sure. Whatever you need.' But that's not *real* support. That allows the delay to accumulate and accumulate until the project fails or racks up extra expenses. Am I right?"

Heads nodded, so I said, "Here's your new rule: no project leader can miss a milestone on their project. Period. Nonnegotiable."

"What!"

"Face it: by the time you get around to announcing the lag, the project is already behind schedule, so it's already too late to fix anything without getting even further behind. *Independent* decisions that should be *team* decisions hold everyone else hostage to your ineffectiveness. Of course, projects do run into problems. You must surface any issue that might lead to missing a milestone. Remember, there's no shame in surfacing a breakdown or problem the project team can't resolve. You are the brightest leaders in this company. You have the breadth of knowledge, critical thinking, and creativity needed to resolve those breakdowns. Just think of the solutions you've already come up with together. If the project team can't come up with a solution, the full-leadership team as owners can push back the milestone dates—completely aware of how that will impact the project and organization.

"Based on the new rule, then," I finished, "an effective leader is not someone who can and does solve all problems by themselves. An effective leader is someone who raises challenges *soon enough* for the entire team to solve the problem."

The idea made them a little nervous, but they all liked it. They changed their meeting process from giving project updates and individual reports to raising and immediately resolving challenges on their primary and secondary priorities. At the next full, senior-and-middle-managers-together meeting, the SLT communicated their Purpose Statement and the seven top organizational priorities so everyone had a clear sense of direction. In fact, one middle manager said, "Now I see where I fit with each of those priorities and how my other continuous-improvement projects support them."

"This is so helpful," another agreed, "that I want to share it with my entire department, so they can see what we're doing to keep our doors open."

"We'll share the purpose and these seven priorities with everyone in our next 'all-hands' meeting," the CEO promised, "so please support that presentation in your team meetings. We also plan to release quarterly updates to keep everyone aligned with our progress."

Within a single year, the medical center was operating in the black. Several quality and patient-satisfaction scores improved, so reimbursements rose. Turnover and vacancies declined. Silos all but disappeared. In the second year, with their tracked results ranking them near the top of all magnet hospitals based on patient-care standards, BMC applied to be a Magnet Medical Center.

B State Accountability

Real integrity is doing the right thing, knowing that nobody's going to know whether you did it or not.

–Oprah Winfrey

I was a pioneer in the accountability movement that made organizations realize why all employees from the plant floor to the C-suite had to own the results of their work. As organizations got on the bandwagon, they introduced "cascading accountability," which deconstructed company strategic plans into specific objectives for each team and, ultimately, each individual. Even today, experts and leaders mostly approach accountability as trickling down to *individual* feedback, *individual* problem-solving, and *individual* goals. In fact, one popular consulting group's accountability model is "Recognize the problem, own the problem, fix the problem." It's all about each person figuring things out on their own—an approach that fosters fragmentation and silos.

While cascading accountability was a good start for its time, it easily fosters an activity-driven (rather than outcome-driven) culture. It lets people waste time on nonpriority issues and ignores the interdependence needed for effective coordination and cross-functional problem-solving and decision-making. Everyone might be busy doing their part, but the organization still does not achieve its desired results because cascading/individual accountability *reacts* to the company's strategic plan rather than *proactively* driving the company's transformation. It demands a focus on the past and present, not the future, so the organization cannot create a culture of accountability that moves it forward in today's fast-changing business environment.

And the company remains stuck in its A State.

B State accountability looks, feels, and acts quite differently. Purpose driven, it serves a cause greater than any individual or even their functional area. "It's not a promise but a process to achieve goals and get better results on a continual basis," according to Annie Hyman Pratt, former CEO of the Coffee Bean & Tea Leaf and now CEO of IMPAQ Entrepreneur. B State accountability flourishes in any environment where people can *count on each other's* attitudes, behaviors, and actions to produce their shared and sustainable desired results. Everyone operates together at the top of the triangle when firefighters address out-of-control blazes, military units defend vulnerable villages, and people support each other in the aftermath of massive floods or fires. In the B State business, everyone pitches in for a common purpose.

In the workplace, "accountable for activity" is replaced by "achieve results"—not just any results, but those set by leadership to optimize sustained success and minimize resource expenditure. People freely offer help, check in on each other, and are dedicated to each other's success, not just their own. B State leverages people's effort, time, and health to realize metrics or goals without leaving "injured" bodies and departments in their wake. No one can cause breakdowns just to gain attention by heroically fixing them. A B State culture of accountability hinges on three key factors:

1. Clear and high expectations

2. A mistake-safe environment

3. Constant development and constructive feedback

Foster a Mistake-Safe Environment

Accountability is risky. Mistakes are unavoidable along the road to excellence, so committing to perform, change, improve, and excel requires a Proactive Recovery Plan. High comfort never leads to greater accountability, but true safety does—acrobats may not use a net to perform on the high wire, but they use one when they practice!

Set Clear and High Expectations

For safety's sake, everyone must understand the "rules of the game" being played, the criteria for successful execution. What is the purpose? What attitudes, behaviors, actions, self-development, support of others, open communication, and so forth will it take to win?

Provide Constant Development and Constructive Feedback

On-boarding, coaching, mentoring, training, and continuous development are critical from day one to final exit. With everyone's mind-set always on doing one's best, they need constructive, positive feedback from teammates and management, so they can determine and correct whatever went off track. In extreme situations, constructive feedback might even redirect someone to a job for which they are better suited.

When the B State culture of giving people the benefit of the doubt, having each other's back, and focusing on improvement extends into the home, it naturally produces an often-unexpected side effect: better communication and cooperation with spouses, children, and even neighbors.

12

Are You Playing an Amateur or a Professional Game?

If you are going to achieve excellence in big things, you develop the habit in little matters. Excellence is not an exception, it is a prevailing attitude.

−COLIN POWELL

I once met with a leadership team so stuck in the blame game that each team member believed they alone had the right solution to the company's challenges—and they all defended their positions with so much arrogance, aggressiveness, and self-righteousness they left no room for self-awareness, understanding, compassion, or critical thinking.

They represented A State's worst qualities.

I went to bed that night disturbed and frustrated. How could I possibly move such a *stuck* group to the B State, with its open, curious, and excellence-driving energy? By morning, I'd had an epiphany: I would tell them about my amateur and professional baseball experiences. The next time I met with the leadership team, I began by saying, "I may have never made it to the pros, but I learned to be a pro and work with pros. Let me tell you my story."

The Professional versus Amateur Game

My Southern California high school produced several professional baseball players—and many teammates and I hoped to be one of them. We all shared the common dream of a baseball scholarship or an invitation to a pro team. Our coach's ambition was aligned with ours: to make us the best ballplayers possible. To an outsider, that kind of scenario might have seemed like a lot of backbiting competition, hard work, and pressure, but it was the most fun and rewarding thing I did at that point in my life—in fact, it *was* my life. We all worked *together*, not against each other. We didn't compete to beat each other out—we supported each other so everyone got better, not just one or two of us.

Paul was a great fielder, but he swung at the air and struck out a lot, so three of us threw him little stones to build his eye—if he could hit a little stone, surely he could hit the larger baseball. We threw rapidly, one after the other, so he didn't have time to think and learned to react quicker. He grounded out on his first at bat in the next game, but then got a square hit on his next—our team ownership of the problem and support had worked. As Jeff Tweedy, leader of the technically superb, Grammy Award–winning alt-rock/country band Wilco, once told me, "After ten years with the group, I finally feel like a success because every member of my band is a better musician than me."

If we don't all win, nobody wins. That "hard work and pressure" felt more like hard play and desire! We all wanted to win ball games and be the best we could be—without taking ourselves too seriously or feeling any malice or jealousy. We laughed with each other and at ourselves.

I stopped playing ball for a few years after my dream of making the pros got shattered, but when I realized how much I missed it, I signed up for a men's community softball league. Relaxed and confident in my skills, I looked forward to the same camaraderie I'd had in high school. I thought, *We're all just playing for the fun of the game . . . there's no pressure to become a professional. This is gonna be great.*

But by the third game, I was disheartened. Instead of having fun, the players blamed each other for not being good enough—even though everyone was an amateur! Some egotistically feigned having professional skills, despite their sloppy play. I quit after the first season. Their unhealthy competition and lack of sportsmanship kept them completely stuck in their A State.

I ended the story with, "The feeling I had on the softball team is exactly what I feel from you and other organizations that struggle to be better, but are stuck in the negative, amateurish culture of blame and punishment."

Suddenly, everyone in the room looked like they'd been caught with their hand in the cookie jar.

"The first huge difference between amateur and professional behavior," I went on, "was purpose. Everyone on our 'professionally oriented' high school team had two purposes—to win and to become the best ballplayer they could possibly be. We didn't have a mission statement or a list of core values; we just had an inner desire. But the community players only wanted to win ball games and to be the 'star that saved the day.' Nobody thought they needed to learn or practice or do anything new or different. Every game was a competition not only against the other team, but against each other. The players figured all they had to do was show up, play—and let everyone admire their talent.

"From my vantage point, you folks are doing the same thing—aren't you? Don't worry, you're not alone. I see this in every A State organization. Managers and nonmanagers alike consider themselves 'experts,' regardless of their actual performance. Everyone believes they, and they alone, have the right answers. No one is ever *truly* open to developing new skills, or improving their performance, or even hearing other people's ideas. Oh, they may pretend they are, but they never change. They claim their 'years of experience'—or maybe some old training program—proves their expertise.

"In a B State organization, your counterparts always work to be better. They not only attend development programs, but constantly talk to each other about making small changes to improve customer service, efficiency, and effectiveness—not just in formal meetings, but even when they pass each other in the hallway. I overheard one of those exchanges. The first manager said, 'The transition between my department and yours didn't go very smoothly. Can we set up a time to figure out how to fix that for the next time?' The second person said, 'Yeah, I noticed the same thing. Let's meet later today to work out a better process and handoff.'"

I looked around the group. "Can you see anyone here, in this room, having that kind of conversation today? A few minutes later, I overheard another manager say, 'Dave, my communication with you the other day was unclear and abrupt. I'm sorry about that—I'll work on doing better in the future. Please feel free to give me feedback when I don't communicate well with you.' The employee said, 'Thanks. Based on your tone I wasn't sure if I had done something wrong, but I knew you were dealing with a lot that day. I really appreciate you coming back to me about it.'

"I don't think I need to ask if you've ever had that kind of conversation, either. I'll just say the second biggest difference between professional and amateur teams is support. Pros constantly support each other without blame. They recognize everyone is human, everyone makes mistakes, and everyone has areas they need to improve, so they always have each other's back and give each other the benefit of the doubt—even when they must have a difficult conversation because someone isn't performing up to their potential. They don't accuse—they're understanding, supportive, and *actively* helpful. They take the time and energy to boost the other person's play or functionality."

After a short silence, one of the SLT members said, "That's definitely not what we do."

"I figured it wasn't," I said. "I figure you have the same issues people have at all levels in organizations like yours. Managers blame employees for not working hard enough. Employees blame managers for not providing clear expectations or for playing favorites. When a breakdown occurs, one person—or manager or department—blames another. On the rare occasion when someone tries to make things better, they're met with criticism or 'crickets.' Does any of that sound familiar?"

My point was proven by their silence.

"B State teams, on the other hand, openly discuss breakdowns, accept that mistakes can happen, and work out execution flaws without pointing fingers. One organization created pairs of managers based on their respective skill-set gaps—someone good at communication but poor at budgeting was matched with someone excellent at budgeting but not communicating. The duos spent a year helping and mentoring each other, and then were evaluated as both mentors and mentees."

"And how did that work out?" someone asked.

"Very well. Everyone not only raised their competency, but developed a trust and respect for their partner and learned to access his or her strengths rather than try to bulldoze through problems on their own without really knowing what they were doing."

People sat up straighter here and there. Some even exchanged glances.

"The third difference between amateurs and pros," I went on, "involves setting clear expectations for results *and* behaviors. My high school coach did that at the beginning of the season. He gave us the discipline, safe practices, personal character, teamwork, and good citizenship standards he expected from us. We had to show up on time, help each other between practices, and participate in other school-sponsored activities—with no exceptions for anyone, whether we were one of the top players or just a bench sitter. Those weren't arbitrary behaviors—they were meant to increase our competence, confidence, and sense of family. Anyone who didn't comply had to sit out for part of the next game or do *extra* physical activity, which actually helped build our strength. If Coach heard us put down another ballplayer, we had to run laps—a lot of them—then partner with that person until we demonstrated our active support and kindness to each other. He was not only teaching us baseball; he was showing us how to interact effectively even in difficult situations—and we learned it all on the field, not in separate workshops.

"Every professional sport has the same level of expectations. Ron Rivera, head coach of the Carolina Panthers football team, instituted a dress code. All his players had to wear ties on the bus to their games—even his star quarterback, Cam Newton. When Newton climbed on the bus before a major end-of-season game without a tie, Rivera benched him, even though they were still trying to make the playoffs! Afterwards, Newton admitted Rivera made the right decision. Now, let me ask you this—how well do you set clear, nonnegotiable behaviors and hold yourself and each other to them?"

"We talk about desired behaviors a lot," one team member said, "but it's pretty much just talk. No one holds anyone else accountable for adhering to them. In fact, we've even created agreements to support each other, but we never follow up on those, either."

"We definitely haven't been as committed as your coach," someone else added.

"And that brings us to the fourth difference between amateurs and pros," I said. "A willingness to change, whether that means changing processes, approaches to the game, or even positions on the team. On our 'pro' team, we changed things weekly based on identified weaknesses, strategies for winning the next game, or injuries. Everyone was willing to change their position, or role, to support our mutual success. I was a pitcher, but not the best one we had, so one year, Coach had me play second base, a new position for me. Even though I loved and was most comfortable pitching, I didn't complain. I just spent extra time learning second base and did the best I could. By the way, one of the pitchers who replaced me, Dennis Lamp, went on to pitch for the Chicago Cubs and Toronto Blue Jays. But on the softball team, everyone 'owned' their position—with pride, ego, and arrogance. 'I'm a shortstop—I'm not going to play outfield! I don't care if Gary is out sick. Get someone else!'"

"Why should *I* have to worry about *your* shipping problems?" a team member muttered. "That's not my department."

That remark pretty much summed up this typical, amateur A State organization. It put in more time and effort trying to overcome resistance and get people's buy-in on a change than it spent helping them understand the benefits of the change—even when it was initiated by the CEO. A simple modification that would take two weeks to implement in another company took these people six months! How much more stuck could they be?

But I'd apparently struck a nerve, exactly as I'd hoped. Several team members shared their own sports and music experiences. They, too, had youthful hopes of a professional career and remembered the fun of working super hard in a "professional" environment of support, dedication, and learning. Others talked about when the organization was smaller and just trying to survive. "We operated a lot more like a professional organization than we do today," someone commented.

"You know," someone else said, "on my last job, we had many of the same issues we have here, but we operated more like professionals whenever there was a crisis to get through."

"People are always more unified during a crisis," I said. "Crisis gives them an unavoidable common purpose; they have no choice but to support each other, be willing to change, or play any role required. That's why so many normal people become heroes during disasters. We all instinctively know we have to work together to get through to the other side."

"We do that during a crisis here, too. Everyone 'drops their ego and entourage at the door,'" another team member said, quoting the famous sign Quincy Jones put up over the studio door before the "We Are the World" recording session. In the end, the team not only committed to adopting more professional behaviors and attitudes, but also decided to develop a training program that shared my story and their professionalism commitment with *all* management levels.

Professional B State Culture Is *Fun!*

There is no greatness without a passion to be great,
whether it's the aspiration of an athlete or an artist,
a scientist, a parent, or a businessperson.

—Anthony Robbins

It's *fun* to be on a "winning" team that makes a positive difference to a cause or purpose greater than mere ego gratification. It's fun striving to be the best we can be. It's fun to learn other people's jobs, to support them as they grow and learn to be better at their craft, and to offer innovative solutions to old problems.

Helping a fellow team member when they drop the ball or make a mistake builds both individual character and team support. When we stand up for ourselves and voice our opinion—when we share our difficulties, questions, and needs for help—we position ourselves as self-confident professionals who promote (and expect) a compassionate environment in which everyone works to improve and be successful. In a professional B State environment—be it business, athletics, music, or family—we trust others to not use our vulnerabilities against us, but to support us as we move forward in our improvement process.

This kind of healthy environment does not come from written mission statements or core values. It only comes from leaders who set reasonable, achievable, yet high-performance individual and team behaviors.

13

The Professional B State Culture

Amateurs practice until they get it right;
professionals practice until they can't get it wrong.

—KENNETH VAN BARTHOLD

No matter what kind of company or their current level of A State, I usually give everyone in my foundational workshop a puzzle to complete with very clear directions about how to complete it. "Before we start," I say, even though most people have already begun figuring out the answer on their own, "I want to make sure everybody is clear on the assignment. Raise your hand if you understand the desired outcome."

That stops them, at least long enough for everyone to raise their hand.

"You just fell into the first trap! How can you understand the desired outcome if I haven't given it to you yet?"

Pencils drop around the room.

"Don't feel too bad," I always go on. "It's very common for people like us, who accept and delegate tasks, to think that *understanding the task* is the same thing as understanding the *desired outcome*—but they're completely different. Plus, you all made an assumption about the task that, if true, would make this assignment a struggle to complete. But it's not true, so you've fabricated exactly the kind of struggle we often see in businesses.

"The desired outcome, which I'll present in a moment, demands higher-level performance, but will be easier to achieve if you all dedicate yourselves to it. Now, when have you ever *raised* performance standards in your organization that made it *easier* to accomplish the desired results? Never! Higher standards always mean more tasks and more work, right? Wrong! So how many of you want to hear *this* desired outcome, which will raise expectations yet make it easier to accomplish?"

After everyone nods or raises their hand, I tell them, "The desired outcome is for every person in the room to demonstrate the correct answer on their page within three minutes. If even only one person doesn't have the answer on their page, the whole room fails. If you get the correct answer but the person next to you doesn't, you fail. If your whole table gets the correct answer but a single person on the other side of the room doesn't, you still fail. The only way to win is for everyone to get the correct answer. Ready? One, two, three . . . go."

I start my stopwatch.

The response is always the same, regardless of country, culture, or type of organization. At least one person suddenly asks the room, "Anyone have the answer?" Then another person spontaneously jumps up, using the flip chart at the front of the room to demonstrate and teach the answer to everyone.

The room buzzes as they share information and help each other solve the puzzle. People walk over to other tables to make sure everyone has the correct answer. Those who struggle try to copy it from someone else's page—but others quickly discover their difficulty and help them write it down correctly. The energy is high, everyone is having fun—and whether twenty-five or five hundred people are in the room, when I say, "Time's up! Show me your solution," they all hold up their workbooks with the correct answer.

"Give yourselves a hand! You guys completed the exercise."

After they congratulate themselves, I say, "Want to know what you really accomplished? I didn't give you any instructions or conduct a workshop on team building, communication, or quality control—yet you naturally demonstrated all those qualities because your focus was on the desired outcome, not on your own performance. You didn't need 'guidelines for good participation.' I didn't have to encourage or motivate anybody to take initiative. You didn't need to clarify your values or learn if the person next to you was a 'driver' or a 'mediator.' Want to see something even more amazing?"

"Yes!" "Yeah!" "Absolutely!"

"How many of you made mistakes before getting it right?" Usually, about three-quarters of the people raise their hands.

"Who cares? No one! There was no 'get it right the first time,' provided you all got it right within the three minutes. There was no shame, criticism, or blame—just support! And it didn't matter who gave the answer, did it? It could have been a manager, an employee—anyone. Anyone learn anything from this activity?"

Everybody chuckles and raises their hands.

"Oops! Sorry! I forgot to create a 'learning environment' first!"

Once they stop laughing, I say, "When you are outcome driven, you want to learn and better yourself to successfully achieve your outcome. You don't need someone to motivate you—you're inspired to succeed. Now, what was your assumption before I explained the desired outcome?"

"I have to solve the puzzle by myself."

"Where did you learn to make that assumption?"

"In school."

"Of course. And when you were in school and you shared your answer with someone else, what was that called?"

"Cheating!"

The "Game" of School versus the "Game" of Business

Most of us spent at least twelve years in school—many of us spent a good many more. The purpose of going to school was to learn. You didn't have to like it, but you had to get through it. Some of us had an easier time and didn't really have to study. Others studied a lot yet still struggled to get good grades. The school gave tests to determine whether you were learning. You had to take them by yourself because a group test couldn't determine what you knew versus the other people in the group.

The school "game" ensured individual learning. The only way to "win" was to do your homework (alone), study well (also alone), and prove your knowledge by testing well (rigidly enforced alone). Individual effort was paramount—and cheaters were punished.

The business "game" is the exact opposite of all that. No individual, no matter how high their grad-school GPA, can possibly fulfill an organization's purpose of satisfying its customers in the most cost-effective manner possible on their own. Every organization succeeds through its *collective* efforts. The person who takes your order and delivers your meal in a drive-through is not the same person who cooks it. The individual who prepares the food depends on whoever orders the supplies and ingredients. Each person must carry out their role effectively, but it takes the whole team to satisfy your desired outcome of a well-constructed bacon cheeseburger.

Any CEO will readily admit they didn't build their organization strictly through their own individual efforts. They drew upon advisors, consultants, colleagues, and outside networks. They learned and gained innovative ideas from others—they recognized that they stood on the shoulders of all those who had come before them.

What schoolteachers call "cheating," business leaders call "smart."

Business Isn't "Clean"

When young adults first enter the workplace, they seldom realize their careers will follow a "tiered development" that relies on those "smart" team efforts, otherwise known as collective execution.

- Tier 1: Learn job and culture of the company.

- Tier 2: Develop new Team Habits of Collective Execution with other team members.

- Tier 3: Develop skills and competencies through workshops, mentoring, and/or coaching to refine their individual and Team Habits.

- Tier 4: Apply skills to improve processes and refine Team Habits of Collective Execution with cross-functional team members.

- Tier 5: Build self-awareness and remove limiting beliefs and emotional reactions through coaching and mentoring.

The sole focus for young new employees is typically on getting and doing the job—not on how to be a team player, deal with inefficient operational bureaucracy, or navigate through conflicting personalities, expectations, and priorities. Consequently, they often get frustrated and demoralized and either quit, complain incessantly until they're fired, or "change careers to look for their passion" when they make mistakes, clash with their fellow workers, or don't complete assignments. The ones who do successfully navigate those challenges often irrationally believe they'll get promoted at the end of a year, the way they advanced from one grade to the next every year if they didn't flunk out.

But when people gain the expertise to do their job well and navigate the challenges of their organization, their next step is *not* a promotion—it's accepting the opportunity to refine their individual and Team Habits, so they can demonstrate greater speed, adaptability, and proficiency under stress and change.

That's the business "game." It's not about being a lone-wolf hero; it's about being an effective and innovative team player.

How I Learned to Stop Being a Hero

I used to like the challenge of solving problems, so when my team surfaced an issue several years ago, I secluded myself in my office and set to work. Even I was amazed and impressed at how quickly I solved it. Thirty minutes later, I left my office to share my brilliant solution with my team. I'll never forget the looks on their faces.

"Uh . . . we solved that about fifteen minutes ago by calling one of our outside experts," one person said. "We're already on to our next problem."

"By the way, Mark," someone added sarcastically, "thanks for your efforts."

We all—well, my team—had a good laugh. When I got over myself a few minutes later, I laughed too.

That's how effective business works. Organizations purposefully engage their resources, talents, and teams into critical-thinking networks that solve problems and reach new levels of excellence. Individual, siloed "heroes" need not apply—although many old-school managers and high-functioning employees still hang on to their silo mentality. Just think about the breakdowns in your own organization that result from lack of information, poor coordination, or problems that don't get surfaced until they become crises and negatively impact everyone. Classic A State.

This scenario is just one more reason why the B State organization utilizes "*collective execution*" rather than "individual stars" to achieve high performance and optimal customer satisfaction. My wife and I had a great B State customer experience when we purchased a Tesla. Every team member—seven different individuals from purchase to delivery—demonstrated their company's culture of high-performance "collective execution."

They answered our questions. They cared enough to share their honest opinions—even if that meant we spent less on extra features. And they kept us in the loop as various individual team members coordinated the different purchase and delivery stages. Was it a perfect experience?

No. But yes.

The driver's window didn't work when we got there to pick up the car, so the delivery team member immediately called a technician, who fixed it on the spot. We drove off the lot as super-satisfied customers. Not only did each Tesla team member provide *individual* high performance, but the team as a whole made sure we were fully satisfied.

Classic B State.

The "B State" Began in Sports and Music

Because of my background in sports and music, the financial waste and marginal results produced by so many process-improvement, team-building, and leadership-development workshops used to frustrate me. Even "Lean" process-improvement efforts, while super helpful, didn't resolve the execution breakdowns that stem from conflicting priorities, or poor problem-solving or decision-making, that undermine operational excellence.

"I'm working with an organization that isn't satisfied with their performance-review process," Todd Alexander, a close friend and B State coach in his own consulting practice, once confided in exasperation. "It's created a lot of staff negativity and isn't producing the results they expected. We did a study to figure out why, and discovered only half the managers used the system!"

"So that half got great results," I said, "and the other half didn't, right?"

"Surprisingly, no—using the system wasn't the deciding factor. The managers who only used the process as a check-off list didn't get any better results than the ones who didn't use it at all. Plus, those managers who *didn't* use the system but had regular performance-improvement conversations with their direct reports got just as good results as those who used the system for what it was intended—to stimulate those very conversations. Turns out, the process itself was less important than the *behaviors* it was supposed to generate—which were what *actually* achieved the desired results!"

Like I said—frustrating. We almost never had those kinds of breakdowns when I played baseball, basketball, or drums. And because my mind goes first to questions, I queried myself:

1. Why do businesses spend millions of dollars on workshops to develop people's communication, problem-solving, and teamwork skills, yet none of the top-performing athletic teams and music groups I played with ever sent me to *any* workshop for *any*thing?

2. Why are communication, teamwork, and problem-solving considered "soft skills" in the business world, yet essential "hard" skills in athletic and music groups, where thousands of people see their mistakes?

3. Why do companies expect their people to perform excellently as soon as they complete a training program and know the process, yet professional musicians and athletes—who already have great skills—practice "collective execution" with their peers for hours to prepare for excellent performance?

4. Why do organizations expect everything to go right the first time—and every time—yet athletic teams and music groups *expect* errors and so develop and rehearse recovery plans?

Every professional athlete and musician knows they must take classes to learn the fundamentals, then must rehearse and practice with others to develop the communication, coordination, timing, problem-solving, and decision-making they need to form the *habits* of execution that optimize their performance.

There's nothing "soft," theoretical, or "philosophically ideal" about an athletic or musical performance. Its "measurement of effectiveness" is based solely on whether the team wins the game, or the audience enjoys the performance.

When I first learned to play the drums, my teacher gave me two or three lessons at a time, but I would push myself ahead to learn five to seven, so I got better as fast as possible. Eventually, I rose to first chair in my school band and orchestra. With more lessons and practice, I competed and qualified for "honor band." I thought I was really good—until I auditioned for a local rock group.

Reading music and playing in school groups didn't give me the chops I needed for their level of collective execution. I didn't know how to listen or jam when there was no structure or conductor, and I didn't have the right attack, played too many fills, and couldn't adjust to different song styles. I just didn't fit in! So they kicked me off the drums, acknowledged my technical skill, and told me to just watch and listen for a while. It took me six months of hanging out with the band and practicing on my own to learn how to transform from being a by-the-book player into a street musician. Only then did the band hire me as their drummer.

I got better over the years—not from taking more lessons or going to workshops, but by playing with musicians who were more experienced and better than me. Over time, I developed my chops until I could effectively play as an equal band member at dances and local concerts. Still, I didn't become an *excellent* drummer until we went into the studio to record. That forced us to tighten our performance and rise to a much higher level of perfection, communication, and listening—especially in those days of four-track recording. The bass player and I had to lay down our parts without any melody, harmony, or vocals behind us. We really needed every little corner and wiggle of a song in our heads and under our hands.

To prepare, the band played five-hour club gigs five days a week and practiced on our days off—while I still carried a full load of college courses! We all improved significantly, and I came to truly understand the importance of "team habits." Playing well wasn't enough; playing well *together* is what made us better and better—and improving "collective execution" never ends. It was all about tiered development, the process of constantly rising to ever-higher levels of excellence, which leads to ever-higher levels of challenge.

High-Performing Team Habits

My high-performance music and athletic skills were not based on any single theory, set of rules, process, or workshop, but rather on the band or team giving its best collective performance despite constraints or individual competencies. Once we reached optimal execution, we practiced it repeatedly, so it became a "team habit." That way, when people were stressed or overwhelmed, no one had to *think* about what to do—it was *automatic*! No one on my school baseball team, for example, had to think twice about what to do to make a double play. We practiced it so much that our *collective execution* became a solid, smooth, *automatic* team habit without *thought* or *fumbles*.

All athletic teams think and practice the same way. The former San Francisco 49ers quarterback Joe Montana once said, "I only work on building my own skills during the off-season. During regular play, I focus on our team's execution because that's what wins ball games—not how well Joe Montana plays. If I change how I play during the on-season, it'll throw off the rest of the team's timing and coordination, and we'll lose games."

Could anything be clearer about the difference between optimizing individual performance and collective execution? Only collective execution wins ball games.

14

The Missing Link: Team Habits

The difference between an amateur and a professional
is in their habits . . . We can never free ourselves from habit.
But we can replace bad habits with good ones.

—STEVEN PRESSFIELD

Anne was frustrated. Her manufacturing plant hadn't made any significant improvement for seven years despite the many good, committed people on her management team. As in so many A State organizations, everyone performed well individually, but not together.

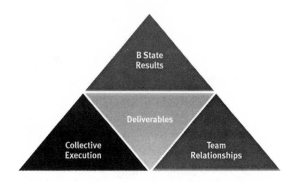

Figure 11: B State Implementation Model

"If I can't bring about the necessary changes to improve our bottom line," she told me, "my CEO will replace me. We have two major issues: incredible resistance whenever we try to implement change—and a lot of those resisters report to people in corporate, not to my senior management team, which blocks our efforts—and alignment. We're viewed as a group of individual high performers, not as a unified team. I've sent my managers to training programs, communication skill-building workshops, and off-site team-building programs, but none resulted in better alignment or team effectiveness—even though everyone appreciated the different learning experiences! It's as if they all say, 'That was fun! Now, let's get back to business as usual.'"

Once I met with Anne's individual team members and then observed them together in a team meeting, I clearly saw the breakdown's root cause. They were aligned on making decisions, but they didn't take the time to strategize and align on communicating those decisions. One person informed their people immediately, another waited a few weeks, a third brought the matter up in their department's team meeting, while a fourth just sent out an email. Naturally, confusion ensued—why *wouldn't* their direct reports question and resist change?

What Habits Are Important to You?

Talent wins games, but teamwork and
intelligence wins championships.

–Michael Jordan

Before I started working with Anne's team to develop a B State Picture of Success, one member asked, "Can't our Picture of Success just be, 'We want to be the best manufacturing division in the corporation'?"

"Sure!" I agreed. "You can say that—but it doesn't provide any direction on what you, as leaders, must do differently to produce the effective systems necessary to *become* the best manufacturing division. What good is having one more slogan to hang on the wall when you have no road map or accountability to do anything differently?"

"Oh. Okay. I guess that makes sense."

The senior management team (SMT) created a Picture of Success with many "do differently" behaviors, and then identified thirteen key "qualities" of collective execution critical to their success. Four of the thirteen included:

1. Openly surface and solve problems in a cross-functional manner.

2. Ensure quality in every production step.

3. Establish effective cross-functional coordination and communication to eliminate breakdowns.

4. Communicate as a unified, "one voice" team to plant personnel and corporate headquarters.

"Okay, good!" someone said. "Now, let's create strategies, goals, and actions, and get back to business!"

That's a common reaction at this point, but it's also a trap that leads right back to being stuck, because whatever we produce is the result of the action we took to produce it. Yes, that's circular, but it's also inescapable. If a team creates a new set of strategies, priorities, and actions *without* changing their ineffective mind-set and approach—in other words, if they use their same old dysfunctional A State behaviors to implement those shiny new action plans—they'll end up exactly where they started: still dysfunctional, still in the same A State.

Let me put it another way. If someone habitually only brushes their teeth every few days, that habit will eventually generate tooth and gum problems. Cause and effect. Inescapable. No one can have healthy gums and teeth if they don't *make it a daily habit* to take care of their gums and teeth.

A friend of mine found this out the hard way. "Your gums have receded to a dangerously low level," his dentist said during a normal checkup. "If you don't want to lose your teeth, we'll have to do a special cleaning that goes under your gums and into the cracks. It's one thousand dollars, but if we don't do it now, we might as well start fitting you for dentures."

"A thousand dollars for a one-time cleaning? I don't disagree with your diagnosis, Doc, but we both know one cleaning won't solve the problem. I must change the way I take care of my teeth. Give me three months. If they're still in the same bad shape then, I'll cough up the money. But let me see what I can do on my own."

He immediately began a new tooth-care regimen. He brushed and flossed twice a day, used gum stimulators after each meal, and rinsed his mouth before bed with special mouthwash. He might have missed a session here or there, but he stuck with the regimen until it became part of his daily routine.

A habit.

It didn't require new skills—he just had to replace his old habit with a new one. That's how we change our habits: not by going for more training or learning new skills or even gaining greater awareness. We simply replace one set of ingrained behaviors with another.

At his next three-month checkup, the dentist was shocked. My friend's gums and teeth were in great shape. He no longer needed the $1,000 cleaning.

Team Habits for Collective Execution

I told this story to the SMT that wanted to "just get going" now that they had their Picture of Success. "Most of us are used to changing our individual habits for the better, for ourselves," I said. "But we're talking about changing your *team* habits, not your personal ones—and so far, you haven't done anything to improve the team's collective execution because you haven't changed the team habits that got you stuck in the first place! All you've done is picture how you want things to be and surface some execution qualities necessary to achieve that picture. That's not enough. You haven't *changed* or even *planned* to change *anything*. So let's look at those thirteen qualities a little closer."

I scanned the room. "I need thirteen volunteers, one to describe, in detail, each of the thirteen essential qualities you've identified. This is not a theoretical exercise. I want you to be very specific about what you need to do *differently* to optimize performance. What are the *specific* behaviors, in a logical process, that are *different* from your current way of doing things?"

Most of the thirteen volunteers found the exercise very challenging. They'd never had to be clear about their expectations before, *and* create a detailed scenario of what fulfilling those expectations would look like when the team did, indeed, lead the "best manufacturing plant in the company." When they finished, we put each statement on a flip-chart page and posted them on the walls around the room, so everyone could view them individually—then the SMT reviewed and modified them *as a team*. They kept rewriting, using everyone's collective input, until everyone was clear, in agreement, and aligned with each statement—and had rated their current performance based on that stated criterion.

They quickly identified a weakness in the fourth bullet, "Communicate as a unified, 'one voice' team with plant personnel and corporate headquarters." The volunteer had originally written:

> After decisions are made, we agree on the talking points
> of our message in order to demonstrate alignment to our
> decisions or to changes we are implementing.

While his statement was clear and represented specific behaviors, the rest of the team didn't feel it went far enough to ensure unified communication. Together, they tweaked it until they reached consensus on the statement below. Yes, it's much longer, but it provides a clearer, more specific expectation for everyone to follow.

> After decisions are made, we agree on the talking points
> of our message in order to optimize the response we get
> from others to our decisions or to changes we are imple-
> menting. We agree on the timing, mode, and method of
> our communication. If there need to be exceptions made
> in how we deliver our message based on the constraints

of our working environment, we discuss those as a team and develop a strategy that will not compromise effective implementation. We brainstorm possible questions or resistance that we could receive from others in order to develop agreed-upon responses for consistency. Even when we disagree with a decision, we represent the team in our communication, not just ourselves. Finally, we collect information about the responses we get, so that we can prepare a secondary communication if necessary.

On a scale of 1 to 7, with 7 = high performance and 1 = low, the team rated themselves at 1.5 on this quality. They were right: this particular Team Habit—or lack thereof—was a major weakness.

We continued the same process for the other twelve Team Habits. While the process was a bit tedious, the group felt, for the first time, that they were clearly aligned on how they would function as a management team.

"In past team-building programs," one team member almost gushed, "we solved puzzles together, built things, and created action plans. But this time, we developed different, practical ways to produce better results."

I wrote a number column from 7 to 1 on a new flip-chart page. "Okay, look around at all the pages on the wall. What's your average score?"

"Two."

I circled 2 on the column. "Do you remember the test you took to accept your Picture of Success paragraph?" I asked, adding another descending-number column, this time from 5 to 1. "What was your score on that paragraph?"

"Two!"

I circled 2 on the second column. Then I drew a line between the columns. "Look," I said. "You're perfectly aligned with yourselves. The 'stretch' of your Team Habits is consistent with the 'stretch' of your Picture of Success. But your Picture of Success is too general—you cannot achieve it. In fact, most groups stop looking at the document soon after they create it, which is why they think it's a waste of time. But you *can* improve your Team Habits to develop high-performing *Collective Execution*. When your habits rise to a five or six, you'll find you are, by definition, living your Picture of Success. Your new Team Habits of Collective Execution are the criteria that will get you to your Picture of Success."

I paused until I saw their eyes refocus. People are always blown away by the link between their dreams and the new behaviors they can adopt to achieve those dreams. When they were ready, I said, "You've done great work so far, but you cannot change thirteen habits all at the same time. I want you to each select the three Team Habits you think are most important to achieve your new B State business priorities. Make sure one of those three also directly improves your Team Relationships."

Using the same weighted rank-ordering process, they prioritized:

1. Communicate as a unified, "one voice" team.

2. Support our direct reports to achieve desired outcomes without excuses.

3. Make fearless, inclusive, action-oriented, and timely decisions.

They formed task forces for each identified habit and created recommendations. Then the entire SMT modified and agreed to each recommendation.

"Excellent," I said. "You are all accountable for implementing these behaviors and actions. Your task forces will review how everyone adheres to them at least once a month so they can surface any breakdowns and bring them to the team for resolution. Now, if you successfully adopt these new Team Habits, will it make a significant difference to your team effectiveness? And will that, in turn, make a difference in accomplishing your priorities?"

"Yes!"

"Making these changes will have a huge impact on our business!"

The SMT's reputation changed among its direct reports over the next two months. Because they now communicated with one voice, they were viewed as solid, aligned, and consistent. Resistance became futile. Employees could no longer play senior managers against each other—no matter who they talked to, they got the same response.

One influential person tested the team's will by complaining about a particular change to two different senior managers, neither of whom was his direct manager. Both not only supported the change, they provided him with identical copies of the same journal article that discussed the change's efficacy. Then his direct manager, anticipating his resistance, emailed him the same article. None of the three managers discussed or strategized their response with each other; it was a spontaneous example of them all being at the top of the triangle—so the employee had no choice but to capitulate.

"I already received this article twice," he emailed his direct manager, "and I'm on board with the change."

Within six months, the fully aligned SMT successfully implemented several important quality, safety, and morale-boosting changes they had previously failed to achieve. The next time the CEO visited Anne's plant, he said, "I've never seen an organization improve performance and morale in such a short time—especially considering where you started and your history of nonmovement. Congratulations! How did you do it?"

By the end of the year, Anne's plant went from a bottom-level operation to being one of the company's top performers, with its performance a benchmark throughout the organization.

15

Measuring Team Habits of Collective Execution

Good is the enemy of great.

—JIM COLLINS

We measure the effectiveness of business teams' collective execution the way athletic organizations and music groups measure their performance: through sensing how smooth the play is and what results were achieved. This requires a sensitivity well beyond standard business measurements.

A good friend of mine, Tom Boyer, played clarinet with the Cleveland Orchestra. In preparation for a difficult piece, he practiced *a single note* for three hours. The instrument was completely in tune, and he hit the note perfectly, dead center, all three hours. What was he trying to achieve? A beyond-perfect, beyond-measurable vibration, sound, and tonal quality he could only hear with great inner awareness. That's sensitivity beyond standard measurements.

Musicians measure their rhythmic precision and note-accuracy "tightness" before they go into the studio, so they don't waste a lot of time—and a whole lot of money. Since a recording studio has little or no natural reverberation and recording equipment is so sensitive, players must perform *perfectly* on every take, while still capturing the song's emotion. Any professional's level of excellence rises synchronously with their focus on greater accuracy and nuance.

When I talk about how to build awareness and "execution sensitivity" in workshops, I demonstrate the point with a drumming flam. To play a flam, you strike the drum with both sticks together—not exactly at the same time, but so closely, it's hard to hear the space between the strikes. A single strike sounds like "tap." A flam sounds like "trap." I bang the table with my hands and ask participants to tell me which is "tighter" between two different flams—the one that exaggerates the difference between my left and right hand ("tra . . . . p") or the one that doesn't ("tra . . p").

Half the audience usually recognizes the second flam as "tighter" than the first, while the other half hears no difference. I ask them to listen again, but this time make each flam tighter: "trap" versus "tra . p." Most people can hear the first flam as tighter, even though the difference is less negligible. Within minutes of deliberate, careful listening, they gain a higher sensitivity for accuracy and precision.

"Can you imagine how high your performance would become," I ask, "if you were that sensitive and attuned to the accuracy and precision of your organization's coordination, communication, problem-solving, and decision-making?"

Evaluating the Performance of Team Habits

> You may think you are losing when
> you are actually winning if you don't keep score.
>
> —Tracy Quinton

Whether or not they're sensitive to the minutiae that herald beyond-perfect excellence, all organizations measure performance and culture. A State looks *backward* to determine where you are now compared to where you were—an incremental approach to change in which you continually reinforce the past to fix what is stuck. It may help you improve somewhat, but it can never get you to your future Picture of Success.

B State looks *forward* to determine where you *want to be* in your new reality compared to where you are now—which is exactly what I did with Anne's SMT six months after our foundational workshop. First, we reread their Picture of Success so everyone remembered the "stretch" they had created for themselves. Then, with the original scores hidden, they rerated each Team Habit compared to *living* their Picture of Success. Once we assessed the gap between their current state and their Picture of Success, we took out the old scores to see whether it had shrunk.

Ten (77 percent) of the thirteen Team Habits received higher scores, and seven of those (54 percent) rated at least two points higher. There were no declines or lower scores.

The team was shocked—they'd only focused on improving *three* Team Habits! Their huge gain demonstrated the counterintuitive power of prioritization: the less we focus on, the more we accomplish. I've implemented this three-focus tactic with hundreds of teams around the world, and I've seen more than 90 percent achieve breakthrough results of 60 to 80 percent improvement within six months, with 35 to 45 percent of that uptick considered significant.

Team Habits and Relationships

Each member of Anne's SMT completed a fifteen-question survey to assess their relationships at our initial meeting. They took the same survey at the six-month assessment—and, again, were surprised by the results: their average score on all fifteen questions had improved by 48 percent!

- Information Sharing: up 59 percent
- Trust: up 48 percent
- Communication: up 35 percent
- Managing Conflict: up 53 percent

Team members had taken no direct action to make those improvements. No communication skill-building workshops. No "trust" programs. No leadership development. They were all an outgrowth of improving their Team Habits.

That's another universal reality: more than 90 percent of all relationship breakdowns in organizations have nothing to do with relationships—they're about unclear collective-execution expectations! Lack of clarity leaves people to individually interpret what is going on or being asked for. The root cause, of course, is an unaligned management team that doesn't speak with "one voice" or present a "unified message." When they present their different views to others, they merely generate even greater misunderstanding, conflict, and disappointment—conflicts which, if unresolved, automatically turn into *mistrust*: First, people don't trust the *information* they get. Second, they don't trust the *person* giving them the information. As the noise increases, people eventually isolate themselves just so they can focus on their job—creating new silos that add to the confusion.

This cycle is absurdly easy to initiate. Suppose a manager tells his direct report, "I need this right away." The manager means, "Get it to me by the end of the day," but because he doesn't specifically say that, or consider his employee's other priorities, the employee interprets his boss's needs according to his own personal situation: "With everything I'm handling, I can't get to this for two weeks, but I'll make a special effort to get it done in the next few days."

Both end up frustrated and disappointed. The manager thinks the employee isn't responsive and might even be insubordinate, so he no longer trusts the man to get things done according to instruction. Meanwhile, the employee feels his special efforts were disregarded, and so doesn't trust his manager to be reasonable. "Nothing I do is good enough, no matter how much extra effort I put in. How am I supposed to get something done by the end of the day with all the other priority deadlines on my plate? Which one do I *not* get done on time *instead*? And how do I handle the fallout from *that* failure?"

They can get together, apologize, and promise to communicate better next time, but until they address the issue of clear expectations, the problem will persist—just as it does so often in family situations. Does this sound familiar? Parents want chores done on a certain schedule but don't consider the child's homework and study responsibilities. Or a child has an extracurricular activity, but the parents don't have that particular time available. Or a couple plans a weeklong "adventure" wedding, but a close family member doesn't have the time—or funds or ability—to attend.

The real problem is never the relationship, although that's what will suffer from the disconnect. We all form judgments about other people based on a lack of clear expectations or consideration for execution challenges.

"He's not a good team member."

"She's insubordinate."

"He's selfish."

"She only takes, never gives."

"We can't count on her/him/them."

"Maybe we need to hire someone new."

"Maybe I should find a new job where they'll appreciate me."

We create Team Habits to clarify expectations and execution protocols and thus provide people with "rules of engagement" beyond typical RACI (responsible, accountable, consulted, and informed) guidelines or job descriptions.

Meaningful Measurements

Metrics are an outcome of behaviors.

—Eric Larson

A measurement can go up or down yet not be meaningful for drawing conclusions. Retail sales typically go down in January after a great December, for example, but that doesn't mean sales have slowed. To make measurements more meaningful, correlate them to other measurements—in other words, compare last year's January sales to this year's January sales. That negative or positive variation is meaningful.

Most organizations measure business results separately from culture or climate, of course, but I've found a direct correlation between Collective Execution and Team Relationships. When Collective Execution (as measured by rating Team Habit effectiveness) is 60 percent, relationships should improve an average of 15 percent on the B State Team Relationship Assessment. Seventy percent correlates to 25 percent improved relationships, and 80 percent correlates to 35 percent improved relationship scores.

If those balanced correlations aren't maintained, the improvements won't be sustained. A 75 percent Collective Execution improvement with a 15 percent relationship improvement, for example, indicates the team's trust, support, and communication aren't solid enough to avoid using hard work and struggle to get your results. But people get tired of hard work and struggle, so the improved execution won't last. On the other hand, you can use that disconnect to help diagnose the "root cause" problem, the first step toward deriving a satisfactory solution.

A government agency implemented a B State transformation to upgrade their regional and national reputation for results and to improve low morale. The thirty-five-member upper- and middle-management extended-leadership team had lots of experience and expertise—along with an air of arrogance. They did a great job developing their Picture of Success and Team Habits of Collective Execution, and they formed five task forces to improve their execution and achieve results. Six months later, their national organization had recognized them for achieving new performance benchmarks and adopted their newly established systems, which were also implemented in other regions. Their Team Habits improved by 70 percent. But their Team Relationships only improved by 9 percent instead of the 25 percent necessary for sustained results.

The room's energy at that six-month follow-up session was fragmented into pockets. Some groups shared great results, while others remained silent and radiated either neutral or negative energy. When I looked at the B State

Team Relationship Assessment's raw data, I discovered a bimodal trend: the scores were mostly 5s and 6s out of 7—there were hardly any 3s or 4s—but a group of five people consistently scored 1s and 2s for every relationship category. No wonder the room's energy felt disjointed!

The accomplishments, Team Habit improvements, and most relationship improvements all correlated, but they were not possible if the 1s and 2s were accurate. After the team and I reviewed all the data, I said, "Clearly, five of you are negative about this process and have a great deal of influence in the room. However, the team has proven you wrong. They achieved great success by working together, and you can't take it away from them. Now, I don't know who those five specific people are, but the rest of you do. You have enough proof to dispel their claim that the process didn't work, so ignore their negativity and stand behind your success. To those five, I can only say, you have a choice: either get on board with everyone else, or be left behind by the rest of the team."

After the session, two people came up to me separately and said, "Okay, you caught me. I was one of the negativists, and I got your message."

"How did you know this was going on without any interviews or in-depth assessment?" one of the upper managers asked in a shocked voice. "We were afraid you'd only see the good results and not the negativity still prevalent in the group, but you nailed it!"

"That's the impact of correlated measurements," I told him. "A simple fifteen-question survey and the ability to connect the dots."

The other three negative team members turned in their resignations the next day. Even though they were union employees in a government organization that didn't let people go, they voluntarily left when the team's empowerment wiped out their individual and clique power.

Collective Execution Can't Be Perfected, Only Improved

Q: At what point does a professional basketball player get good enough to stop practicing free throws?

A: Never. Pros continue to practice until they retire from the game—and often keep practicing for years, if not decades, afterward.

Q: How experienced do musicians need to get before they stop rehearsing?
A: Just ask the Rolling Stones, who have been playing the same songs for more than fifty years and still rehearse and get in shape before every concert tour.

Q: When should an organization accept "basic" performance levels as good enough?
A: Never—but they often do, falling back on the old saw, "If it ain't broke, don't fix it."

Can you picture Olympic gold-medal sprinter Usain Bolt or Michael Phelps, the most decorated Olympian of all time, having that attitude?

I realized two things at the same time one day as I put down my drum track in a recording studio: (1) "I'm finally good enough to drum on music that will be played on the radio," and (2) "I'll never make it as a professional studio drummer. This is as good as I'm going to get. Funny—I had to get this good to realize my limitations!"

With their Team Habits improvements directly linked to their Collective Execution, Anne's manufacturing plant went from one of the worst in the organization to one of the best inside six months. We continued our six-month assessments with her SMT as their business results and Collective Execution effectiveness continued to improve. They'd taken care of their initial dysfunction by the second assessment and were ready to expand their leadership role, so they added four new strategic and project-management Team Habits to their original list of thirteen.

Team Habits constantly evolve in response to changing demands. What worked yesterday might be inadequate today and completely obsolete tomorrow—which is perfectly natural. After all, we expect different behavior and capacity from a fifteen-year-old than we do from a seven-year-old!

Lower Scores Can Indicate Significant Improvement

During the third assessment, we rerated their now seventeen Team Habits. This time, two went *down*—significantly!

One involved the topic called Information Sharing. The added time crunch from expanding their facility caused several team members to miss meetings, so they weren't getting updates or sharing information as regularly. The team committed to problem-solve this situation at their next weekly meeting. But the second decline was for Proactive Course Correction and Reprioritization, a habit they chose to improve during their last assessment. Naturally, they were quite distraught about their "failure."

"Wait," I piped up quickly. "Before you draw any conclusions about this, let's do a quick analysis. We rate the Team Habits based on your Picture of Success, but to figure out the root causes, we ask a different question: Do you believe your performance on this Team Habit is worse now than it was six months ago?"

"No!" several people exclaimed.

"If anything," one person said, "we're doing much better now than six months ago!"

"Then why did the score go down?"

"Are we doing the wrong things?"

"Do you *think* you're doing the wrong things regarding that habit?"

"No, I don't . . . but the score went down!"

"And that's a problem we sometimes run into with measurements," I assured them. "We can easily draw the wrong conclusions if we take them out of context. Can you think of a reason why the score would go down?"

"Our expectations went up?"

"Yes! Remember the difference between the flams I demonstrated at our first meeting? You've grown more sensitive and attuned to higher performance and execution standards than you were when you initially wrote that habit, just by increasing your focus on improving it. It's an organic change. You didn't need corporate to raise standards or dictate an improved-performance requirement. You didn't even need to discuss it. Your "collective awareness" and standards increased naturally. Congratulations! This is a game changer! You'll never again tolerate the old substandard level of performance you accepted just a year ago!"

"Wow!" someone said. "This is the most fun I've ever had on a job! We're all on the same page, all striving for excellence, all have each other's backs— but we're all still carrying our own weight. I honestly didn't think this was possible two years ago!"

Classic B State.

Collective Execution at Home

"I think I'm heading for divorce if my wife and I can't resolve our differences," one of my CEOs told me out of the blue one day. "Can you help?"

I said I'd try. We met at a local hotel conference room away from his office and their house. They walked in together but wouldn't look at each other. He didn't think his wife would change even if she could. She figured we'd be biased against her and just agree with all his perceptions.

"This is a different process than either of you imagines," I said, "or have experienced with your marriage counselors. We're not going to focus on your problems. Instead, we're going to create a new reality for your marriage."

"Like you did with my management team," the CEO said.

"Yes—but with a twist, because this is personal. Let's start fresh with a B State Picture of Success for your marriage. I want you both, separately, to write several ideal *qualities* of your marriage and partnership, such as respectful communication or forgiveness for mistakes. Whatever your hot buttons are."

Not surprising—to me, anyway—their individual qualities were similar to each other's. They both really did want the same things out of their marriage.

"Okay, now use those qualities as a foundation to write a set of paragraphs that describe the ideal *behaviors* you want to adopt—first with each other, and then as a united front with your children."

For the first time in over a year, they worked as true partners, neither dominating the other. When they finished, they were both excited and proud of what they'd created . . . together. As a team. As a loving couple.

But then the wife shook her head. "This all sounds really good, but what happens when real life shows up? It all goes out the window, and we're back to sniping and bickering."

"Which is why you have to develop new habits," I said. "Like any other team, you two must agree on how you'll address difficult family situations."

"Suppose we do make an agreement," the wife hedged. "What happens when my husband doesn't keep his word?"

"Or you don't keep yours," he retorted.

"First, we have to agree on *what it will look like* to demonstrate the behaviors you just agreed on, or what I call Team Habits. Then, we'll set up a process to review and support each other in changing each of your habits. This will be new for both of you, so neither will be perfect at it right off the bat. You need to support each other."

"What do you mean by 'Team Habits'?" she asked.

"Well, for instance, let's talk about your ideal behavior of him being home for dinner. That will be a major change and challenge for him—a new habit he has to establish for himself. He's committed to *give up* his habit of going out for a few drinks after work, so he *can* be at the dinner table, on time, at least four nights a week. He also committed to let you know by noon if something comes up that prevents him from getting home on time on one of the days you expect him.

"For your part, you agreed to change *your* habit of serving dinner at five thirty, and push it back to six thirty, so he has time to get there—and you agreed to adopt a new habit of *giving him the benefit of the doubt* rather than blame him for not calling earlier when something comes up in the afternoon."

"That sounds good," she admitted.

"And you'll meet once a week to make sure you're both sticking to those agreements. If you're not, you'll discuss the problem and come up with a joint resolution."

They both liked the idea of the follow-up, which had been missing from all the other suggestions and therapies they'd tried. By the time we were finished that day, they had ten new Team Habits for how they'd talk to each other, make decisions, surface problems for resolution, and communicate with "one voice" to their children, other family members, and friends. They each had a different emphasis on what was important, but each new Team Habit consisted of the best qualities of each person. And, as usual, I told them to focus on the three most important habits for the next three months.

That session took place more than ten years prior to this writing—and the couple is still together as I put fingers to keyboard.

16

The Middle-Management Miracle

None of us is as smart as all of us.

–KENNETH H. BLANCHARD

Middle managers are usually experts in their particular function, be it finance, human resources, operations, quality, or information systems. Each has the technical competence and management skills to plan, organize, and improve performance within their functional area. Unfortunately, though, most have little knowledge about how other functional areas work or deal with challenges.

Middle managers' priorities often unknowingly compete with other functional areas. They seldom plan, coordinate, or communicate outside their own silo, so they make decisions without realizing the breakdowns, rework, poor customer service, or unnecessary operating expense they're generating in other areas.

It really isn't their fault—their job, in a standard organizational structure, almost mandates they focus exclusively on optimizing their own functional area. They have no choice but to operate in a silo at the bottom of the B State Consciousness Triangle, where they can command employee loyalty and protect their area and people, but from where they see only their individual piece of the puzzle. They have no idea what the complete picture looks like.

I saw this exact scenario in an international petroleum company that had approximately thirty-five isolated middle managers. The senior team updated them on the organization in a monthly group meeting, then met with their direct reports separately to review performance. The middle managers, in turn, then met with each of their supervisors . . . who met with each of their team leaders . . . who met with each of their team members.

Most organizations continue this "cascading accountability" system all the way down to the lowest employee level—the perfect way to *reinforce* silos at every turn. But no matter how common it is—no matter how many business books or consultants support or advocate this model—cascading accountability can never optimize organizational performance, because organizational performance cannot be optimized from within silos. It's that simple.

The pipeline company had another common challenge as well: many of their senior technical experts—who did their jobs using knowledge based on decades of experience without using current technology—were reaching retirement age, but the company had never developed younger people to replace them. They had run out of time—they had to replace all those years of experience with people who could learn new technology. They gave themselves twelve months to revamp their structure, install new technology and equipment, and change their culture from silo-based to cross-functional teamwork. They would restructure the organization in the first three months, change the processes in the second three, plan the transition to the new equipment in the third, and install the equipment and begin the culture change in the final three months. They figured the culture change would take place *after* all that and require several years to fully implement.

After the first quarter of the change, the SMT members were still stuck on what the new structure would look like. Since they didn't like using outside consultants—after all, they were all very smart engineers who could handle it all on their own—they asked me to facilitate a one-day strategy session, just to get them unstuck.

We clarified their purpose: transform from being "intuition driven and customer reactive" into a customer-responsive, efficient pipeline organization using accurate analytical logistics. Their new business model—change from a cost-plus utility to profit control and volume risk.

"We're very concerned about how our employees will take all these massive changes," one of the senior managers said, "along with having to learn entirely new skill sets."

"Forget about the new structure for a moment," I said. "What's your middle managers' key role change in this transformation?"

"They'll change from leading twenty percent, managing fifty percent, and doing thirty percent to leading seventy percent, managing thirty percent, and doing zero percent."

"Wow, that's huge! What will their new role look like?"

"Ummmmm . . ."

So we brainstormed a list:

- Accountable for planning future business results
- Effective cross-functional coordination, relationships, and problem-solving
- Become logistics experts and develop best practices
- Deliver financial-margin results
- Create short- and medium-range plans to develop current employees and succession plans
- Provide check-and-balance for each other's long-term goals
- Communicate expectations and hold people accountable with effective coaching
- Manage pipeline flow based on multiple customer demands

"Since these are huge changes from their current role," I pointed out, "what do you suspect their fears will be?"

We brainstormed another list, including

- Unrealistic expectations
- "My current 'empire' is being taken apart"

- Lack of qualified staff
- Letting go of "doing"
- Mutiny from their direct reports
- SMT continuing to micromanage them (a cultural norm)
- Lack of commitment to this "flavor of the month" change

"So," I said, "since this is such a radical change, why not do the change radically and put the culture first? The other changes will follow much easier that way."

"That's impossible!" one member blurted out. "We have to be clear on what roles people will have based on the new structure before we can change the culture!"

"Actually, you don't."

Five pairs of eyes stared at me.

"All you need to know," I continued, "is who will likely be on the middle-management team—even if you don't yet know in what position. It's even okay if they don't all make it to the team. You just need to start. Why don't you use your new leadership culture to *guide and manage* the transformation, rather than try to figure this out all on your own. Isn't that what middle management is here for?"

"I don't think they have the strategic and critical thinking skills to lead this change," someone said.

"If you aren't ready to empower your middle managers to lead this change now, what makes you think you'll be willing to empower them in nine months, after you've been controlling them every step of the way?"

"Huh," the business-unit leader said. "You're right. But we have no idea how to set them up to take on such a role."

"It's not as difficult as you think. They just need to become their own unified, cross-functional leadership team. They need their own purpose and to *expand their role* from functional managers to business leaders. In other words, they, too, need to be responsible for the entire success of this change and its business results."

"No."

"I don't think so."

"I'm not even sure that's possible."

"Frankly, I don't think we want to let go of our cascading accountability," one person finally admitted. "It's how we've always worked . . . and I don't think we'll be comfortable giving up that control."

"Okay," I said. "How about if you keep your cascading accountability, but with a focus on middle management as a *team*, not as individuals. Otherwise, you'll end up maintaining your current silos, which will undermine all your carefully laid-out plans."

"You don't know our middle managers," another SMT member protested. "They're terrible with interdepartmental coordination and communication. They constantly blame each other—and us—whenever there's a breakdown. They fight for control and power. It would take months and months—maybe years—to embed the kind of culture change you're talking about. We don't have that kind of time."

"You don't need that kind of time," I countered. "I can guide them through creating their own Picture of Success and Team Habits of Collective Execution specifically for their new and expanded role as change agents and business leaders in a matter of days—not months or even weeks. It'll be the fastest, and possibly the most effective, change you make in this organization."

"That's unrealistic," another manager spoke up. "Our corporate culture-change expert has already proposed a two-to-four-year culture change—if not significantly longer."

"Yeah, that's a common response from traditional change-management consultants," I agreed. "But do you really want to take that much time to implement this business transformation? If we use a B State transformation process rather than a traditional change-management one, we can get this done and get you on to your next three-month plan in a matter of days."

"Oh, really?" the most skeptical SMT member said, smirking. "And how long do you project it will take to turn them into an effective team?"

"Two days."

"Two days! Are you kidding me?"

"Okay, slow down, everyone," the business-unit leader put in. "We can afford two days. But we're not going to trust this process," she said, turning to me, "unless we can test them at the end of the two days to see if they really *can* operate as a team."

"Fair enough. You're all invited to test them with questions about the new structure you haven't been able to solve—or any other implementation challenges. And you're invited to hear them present their responses by the end of the second day."

"Okay!" she said. "We'll decide who will participate in this process and start implementation at the end of the month."

"Perfect!"

One Month Later

The day came. I brought all thirty-five middle managers together in the same room. They thought they were in for another traditional management-training program—they'd done a lot of those together but had never come away thinking of themselves as a single team with a common purpose. After the business-unit leader reviewed the purpose of the organization's change and their new expected role as "change agents" and "business leaders," I took over.

"I want to talk about your new role as leaders. Until now, you've been managing your functional area to achieve performance goals and metrics. Your new *expanded* role is to lead this change and be accountable for the highest levels of operational excellence within this business unit. In other words, you're going to translate your organization's purpose and overall strategy into *collective* improvements that can only be achieved as a team."

"Are you kidding?"

"Hey, my evaluation is based on achieving *my* metrics, not anyone else's."

"There are too many of us to work as a team. Forget it—it can't be done."

"How can we work as a team, when senior management micromanages us?"

The group was evenly mixed between genders, but the resistance came mostly from the women in the group. The men took a more passive stance. They slouched in their chairs with expressions of disbelief or irritation. Ultimately, everyone complained that they were already overworked and had no time or energy to take on a larger role.

I didn't try to change their beliefs—I never try to change anyone's beliefs. I merely reminded them of their two choices. "You can either step up to this empowered role and work together to lead this transformation, or have it controlled and dictated to you by senior management. It will happen either way, so it's your decision. Besides, you can only do your best, given your circumstances. You can't wait for things to be ideal before you show up as leaders. If you support rather than blame each other starting right now, you can at least create a more positive environment while you're facing the new challenges that are about to happen."

They didn't agree—or even understand—but they let me lead them through the first activity: develop their own Picture of Success as change-agent leaders. I used the same process I use with senior management teams—I asked them three questions.

1. What do you want your middle-management team reputation to be with your direct reports and upper management as you lead this major transformation?

2. How will you team with each other to optimize information sharing, problem-solving, communication, and decision-making?

3. What will the results be for your business unit and customers once you lead the change and raise standards of performance and effectiveness?

As usual, the group brainstormed responses focusing on "do differently" behaviors, attitudes, and actions, and then was separated into three groups of about twelve each to write their paragraphs for each question. And—again as usual—each group took about forty-five minutes to complete their paragraphs. Only one of the three groups didn't pass the test and had to fine-tune its paragraph. Paragraph sharing took the typical thirty minutes, and as usual, when all three Picture of Success paragraphs were read, everyone felt they were meaningful, actionable, and an upgrade to their current management role.

In less than three hours, they were excited instead of skeptical, especially since—again, as usual—all the paragraphs read like one person had written them. But even more, they were amazed at how smoothly and quickly it had happened with all thirty-five people in the room. "If we can work this fast going forward," one of the former skeptics said, "this team can accomplish a lot!"

They called themselves the Change Leadership Team (CLT) and adopted this business-leader Picture of Success:

> As the Change Leadership Team, we provide clarity and strategic direction and expectations for each group and individual without demanding perfection. We create an environment of open communication and transparency where we actively remove obstacles and encourage involvement in decision-making. We facilitate and lead business, process, and culture change as a unified and well-coordinated team. We develop and facilitate the success of all employees and ensure the successful delivery of business results. We regularly celebrate individual, team, and organizational success.
>
> We are a collaborative culture that aligns the functional groups toward a common business objective. Teams work together to better understand each other's needs in an open and supportive environment. All team members have a clear understanding of the impacts of their decisions to the bottom line and to each other. We challenge individual thought to achieve business unit goals.

Our relationship with the SMT demonstrates open two-way communication. Mutual trust is earned through the results of our collaborative business actions. We effectively lead by predicting, monitoring, and sharing results of our team's decisions and actions. The SMT views us as a confident, empowered team that effects change.

The benefit to our company as a result of our evolution will be the ability to maximize net margins while becoming the industry's service provider of choice while attracting and retaining top performers. The benefit to our customers is that they will be receiving a predictable service at a reasonable rate. We will accomplish this by clarifying our service offerings, proactively anticipating our customers' needs while building collaborative relationships, eliminating redundancies in our organization, and tracking and measuring results.

They left for lunch energized and excited. When they came back, they used their Picture of Success to develop thirteen Team Habits of Collective Execution—a concept that had been foreign to them just a day earlier. Five of those included the following:

- Understand each other and effectively work together to optimize the business unit's results.
- Actively remove obstacles through open and honest two-way communication.
- Effectively plan, communicate, and lead change based on our B State Picture of Success.
- Ensure inclusive and timely decision-making based on our priorities, B State Picture of Success, and cross-functional impact.

· Provide a predictable service at a reasonable rate through cross-functional collaboration, tracking, and measurement.

That led to writing Team Habits that provided a clear, agreed-upon understanding of expectations, such as this one for "Actively remove obstacles through open and honest two-way communication":

> We immediately and openly surface issues or breakdowns before they become a crisis. We determine all the functional areas impacted by the issues beyond the direct people involved and convene them quickly to discuss alternative solutions. We include our employees in analyzing situations and developing solutions. Based on agreed-upon criteria for making an effective decision, we quickly align on a unified solution. If there is disagreement, we develop a "proactive recovery plan" to address potential breakdowns instead of getting bogged down in analysis paralysis or consensus decision-making. We communicate with "one voice" to others on our decision and implement with ongoing assessment and refinement.

I asked each manager to select their choice of the top four Team Habits to improve during the next six-month period based on supporting the change effort. Using our built-in weighted-ranking process, they chose the following:

1. Effectively plan, communicate, and lead change based on our B State Picture of Success.

2. Understand each other and effectively work together to optimize the business unit's results.

3. Effectively utilize and share resources across the business unit.

4. Effectively manage and monitor shared results.

They created four task forces to develop clear improvement outcomes along with practical, "do differently" recommendations for each new habit. The task forces then shared their recommendations with the rest of the CLT, which challenged the first task force's approach because it relied too much on senior management input, rather than their own CLT's decision-making. The task force promised to redo their recommendation for the next team meeting. The team also asked task force number four to come up with a way for all team members to quickly and easily review results.

Typically, each task force determines its own strategies and recommendations independently from the rest of the team, but all the team members "owned" the strategy and success for all the task forces in this process, so they held each other responsible for implementing their agreed-on recommendations.

The three members of the SMT who came to the session after lunch the second day were impressed with the CLT's Picture of Success and thirteen Team Habits on the walls, but they really came to test the team—as promised.

"We've prepared a set of problems involving our desire to change the structure and implement new processes based on this change effort," one of them stated. "We want recommendations before the end of the day from you as a team. We'll be back later to get your input."

A few middle managers asked some clarifying questions; then the team organized themselves into four cross-functional groups balanced with people who were and were not directly involved in each question. They gave themselves two hours to develop their response and one hour to present it to the CLT for feedback.

After an hour or so, members of each group got up to consult with the other groups about the direction they were taking and solutions they were generating—a remarkable demonstration of the power and efficacy of the

B State. Thirty-five people who, one day earlier, were positive they could not and would not work together now not only worked well in cross-functional groups, but resourced each other in separate groups! They had all completely shattered their silo-behavior comfort zones to operate together at the top of the triangle. Before they made their final presentation, everyone was clear on each other's direction, solution, and presentation.

Even I was amazed.

At 4:00 p.m., the three SMT members returned. Many of the presentations turned into discussions as the senior managers asked critical-thinking questions. They could not help but recognize their middle managers' excellent preparation and ability to speak on each group's work. At 5:30—a half hour longer than planned—the SMT member who'd been the most skeptical and reticent said, "I'm stunned! I'd never have predicted you would work so fast, be so aligned, and have such strong critical thinking behind your responses. You've developed very effective strategies and solutions for something we've been struggling with for three months!"

The SMT group huddled for five minutes, then announced, "Based on your excellent work, we'd like you to continue as a team and propose the organization restructuring within the next month. Are you open to taking on that monster of an assignment?"

The CLT's designated leader looked at his team for confirmation.

"Yes."

The CLT's new restructure, delivered on schedule, included demoting four middle-management positions. The SMT made some small adjustments, but it had a solid reorganization determined and planned for implementation within six weeks—all led by the middle-manager team. The company got back on its original schedule within a month, even though it had been three months behind when I was called in. Even better, business-unit performance increased during the same period, and employee engagement rose. In fact, employees at all levels began turning to each other to resolve differences rather than use the chain of command to run to their manager.

As a result, they transformed their systems, processes, and culture on time, producing greater responsiveness and quality to customers. They expanded their customer base and lowered their operating costs at the same time. This process was so successful, several middle managers were promoted to the SMT—proving, once again, that the B State effectively develops leaders and succession planning.

17

Evolve and Develop Leaders

Tell me and I forget. Teach me and I remember.
Involve me and I learn.

—BENJAMIN FRANKLIN

Most organizations treat team and leadership development as events, for which participants receive certificates or some other form of recognition at the end of the workshop or program. But there is little follow-up or accountability on whether they're applying their new skills to improve performance—especially in the case of "catalog" programs randomly taken as a special interest or at a manager's request.

The better development efforts always impact people's mind-set, attitudes, behaviors, and skills that apply to their whole life, not just their work. They also include a follow-up process complete with internal or external coaching so the person doesn't fall back into old, more comfortable habits. But while all development programs are, by definition, short lived, true development never ends—it keeps evolving as society changes, customer demands increase, and new innovations are discovered.

Unfortunately, most organizations don't invest in readiness for eventualities or natural change once their employees are *"good enough for now."* They may provide workshops for "high potentials," but once those people get promoted into management, they're treated as if they've "arrived"—as if they now can simply handle any new situation, generation of employees, competition increase, or other change. Except for occasional workshops and programs to introduce new techniques and skills, their development effort typically stops, a dangerous step for any organization's evolution.

That's why a B State sustained-success organization continually gets its infrastructure and people *ready* for its next stage of development. Like athletes and musicians, *your* Picture of Success must always be pointed to the *ever-evolving/changing* future. Never accept past success as a reason to stop readying yourself for what's coming. The world constantly reinvents itself, so you must stay in constant learning mode. You must continually work on your individual and team habits to improve your Collective Execution's speed, agility, and accuracy.

Whether the next step is from entrepreneurial effort to established business, medium-sized company to large corporation, national enterprise to global entity—or even consolidation in response to economic pressures—there is *always* a next evolutionary step. If you don't keep pushing forward, you will inevitably slip behind.

When B State Becomes the New A State

A relatively new division in a service-based company had major operational breakdowns. It had hired the best talent, but they were mired in silo and victim behavior. The division's executive team implemented a B State transformation to quickly change their culture, remove players who weren't willing to develop themselves regardless of their tenure, and redesign their processes to produce better results. Their Picture of Success read as follows:

> As Executives, we diligently assess our division's external and corporate environment to develop a responsive "picture of success." We are expert at defining clear roles and expectations, strategies, and direction, in an evolving context of change.
>
> Executives view the organization as a collective of individuals whose unique talents and perspectives are

required for success and need to be activated to improve performance. Executives are committed to talent management. We communicate strategy and decisions with a single voice and do so in a reliable and timely manner. We support mid-management's good habits in execution and accountability. We have proven the capability for sustaining a culture of excellence.

The Executive Team is adept at managing in a matrix structure with Corporate, and we transparently communicate and work together across functions to drive the success of our division. We effectively manage change and resolve conflict in a timely manner. We listen attentively, and actively support popular and unpopular decisions, and take intentional risks to achieve our objectives.

As Executives, we recognize and celebrate each other's successes. We consistently demonstrate the highest levels of trust, respect, and regard for each other, which enables us to have direct, challenging, and difficult conversations. We have effective and proactive recovery plans for times of stress and when workload is overwhelming.

We create and support a high-reliability safety culture that achieves outstanding customer service. Through innovation, shared ownership, and positive esprit de corps, we measure our success by improvements in quality, productivity, employee engagement, operational effectiveness, and positive financial performance. We influence our future by embracing uncertainty, effectively managing change, and being good stewards of our resources to maintain financial sustainability.

Performance improved significantly. A year later, though, one executive still micromanaged her direct reports and maintained an unsafe, fractured environment despite coaching and improvement plans. Her department's disengaged managers still complained constantly, and staff felt both smothered and ignored by their executive. When senior management finally realized they could not move her needle enough, they exited her and hired a new executive from outside of the organization.

By the middle of the second year, they'd become the top-performing division among twelve in their corporation and represented 40 percent, the largest share, of its profitability. Silos were all but eliminated, and middle managers worked well with each other and with executives to resolve challenges—a new core competence for all managers. Employee morale and customer satisfaction were at an all-time high.

Unfortunately, when the company's industry went through a financially challenging time, corporate cost-cutting put a strain on the division. Hiring was frozen, frustrating managers and employees alike, who had to work harder with fewer resources. They could not even replace many positions.

Corporate brought in one of the top four accounting firms to do an operational and financial assessment of the entire company. Their conclusions were announced at the end of September: The goal was to dramatically improve productivity and reduce operating expenses to produce overall savings of 25 percent to 35 percent. In January, the company would centralize responsibility for these initiatives rather than allow each division to operate autonomously. Many functions within each division would be managed at the corporate level.

The Executive Team knew this degree of rapid transformation couldn't be resolved with their standard tools—strategic planning, leadership workshops, or team building—and that they couldn't simply re-create what we'd done together two years earlier, so they brought me back to lead them through *another* B State transformation to replace what had now become their A State.

First up, we developed a new story involving the external drivers, their purpose messaging, and the change priorities to mobilize and inspire their already stressed workforce. All managers expanded their role so the change could happen quickly, successfully, and as painlessly as possible. We ended up creating a new A State/B State comparison of middle-manager and supervisory roles so the Executive Team could set those new expectations. The division leader called me just a week later.

"It's amazing how everybody got engaged just by telling our new story. We've had the least amount of resistance to this change compared to any other we've ever had to implement. People on both management levels are excited about their expanded roles."

Three months later, she called to say, "Our division literally led the change for the entire organization. We were the first to accomplish it; we had the best results—the B State really works! Now we must prepare for centralization."

They'd never operated in a centralized environment before. They didn't understand—or even know—the necessary mind-set or behavior changes they needed to make, and they were already running into operational breakdowns between senior managers and corporate leaders. So I went back once more to guide the senior managers through a new Executive Team Picture of Success. Notice the difference between the original and the one below.

> The Executive Team and leaders are a resource, innovator, and business partner for strategizing Corporate-led changes and early adopters of new systems to improve operational excellence. This is demonstrated by incorporating subject-matter experts in product-line planning and execution. We are viewed as providing systems that consistently provide high reliability in safety, quality, and customer experience and satisfaction. Through this approach, our Business Unit optimizes our role within the Corporation.
>
> The Executive Team is widely viewed as true "servant leaders," consistently responsive to our customers, employees, and each other. Our team is known for its skill in developing, coaching, and mentoring employees at all levels, and as being effective business and product line leaders focused on optimizing the quality and

reliability of our products. We strive to establish clear, high-performing expectations and goals; we generate healthy accountability for timely and effective execution. The Executive Team has a defined brand that is promoted through clear definition, Corporate and internal communication, and role modeling at all levels.

We nurture existing relationships with key Corporate leaders and decision makers and expand each other's relationships within our existing networks. We improve our Business Unit's influence and create a positive perception within the Corporation. We leverage product-line business reviews to position our Executives and leaders as subject-matter experts that influence the direction of the Corporation and develop business plans that reflect Corporate impact.

Our Business Unit leads the Corporation by looking outside of the four walls of our Business Unit and successfully implementing innovative programs, product creation, and delivery that is evidence based and data driven. We continue to involve our professional and local communities to stay ahead of and respond to trends guiding the evolution of our product lines.

"Now this is the kind of strategic focus and thinking I've always wanted to be a part of," one team member said.

"I can't believe how different our Picture of Success is from the previous one," another piped up. "We liked it a lot, but this one is even better and more inspiring."

"Yes," the division president said, "but we never could have gotten here if we hadn't accomplished our previous Picture of Success. It's as if our prior focus got us ready for this dramatic change—which no one could have foreseen."

"That's why I love working in this division!" said one of the corporate members who was part of the team. "We're not bogged down by internal breakdowns and silo behavior. We can address the strategic issues that will help us influence corporate."

Of course, when they changed their Picture of Success, they also had to change their Team Habits of Collective Execution.

"Should we be worried that our old Team Habits will decline?"

I shook my head. "You can always rerate them to see if there's a decline, but think about it—those Team Habits scored between 1 and 3 when you originally created them, but now they get scores of 5 to 7, which means you consistently demonstrate them. That's why we refer to them as *habits*—they're second nature to you now, a true representation of your culture."

"That's so accurate," the president agreed. "I used to wonder what our next Executive Team level needed to be. Now I'm totally clear on how we need to evolve as leaders."

Leaders at Every Level

At a medical center that maintained high levels of accountability, commitment to employee engagement, and leader development, I certified internal facilitators to help every department create their own Picture of Success and Team Habits of Collective Execution—including how to effectively work with other departments and physicians. Each department posted them on their own walls, so anyone who interacted with them would understand their commitments to high performance, teamwork, and improvement, and hold them accountable to model those behaviors. Those "internal customers" then assessed how well they lived up to their posted standards.

Potential new employees received the department's Picture of Success and Team Habits. They typically either looked it over quickly and handed it back, saying something like, "That's great, thanks for showing it to me," or they read it carefully and said, "You really work this way? That's fantastic. This is the kind of team I want to be part of!"

Who would you hire?

Management used the Picture of Success and Team Habits again during the on-boarding process. They also incorporated the Team Habits into their individual-performance evaluation process, since they'd been designed to achieve the highest internal levels of performance, teamwork, and morale possible. Consequently, each department's hiring, on-boarding, team performance, continuous improvement, and individual-performance appraisal was fully integrated. In fact, every employee created a personal Picture of Success that aligned with their department's Picture of Success.

This medical center ultimately became its industry's benchmark. Its CEO spoke around the country about how they achieved their breakthrough patient care, quality, and culture success. They even developed a new revenue stream by offering monthly tours and education to other medical-center administrators. The month I showed up, they had about fifty participants.

A shining example of the B State in action.

The Role of Skill Building and Process Improvement

Sports teams review game tapes every week to identify missed Collective Execution. When the root cause is poorly executed Team Habits, the team spends the next week practicing coordination and team communication to solidify it into a high-performing habit regardless of game pressure. Other times, a play needs to be changed for more effective execution—just like an organization sometimes needs process improvement. Occasionally, an individual just doesn't perform well, so they receive individual coaching/training to reinforce their skills and how to apply them to the team's Collective Execution before they return to team practice.

Skill building and process improvement are critical to evolve any organization, but to effectively improve their desired outcomes, those efforts must directly link to new individual *and* team habits with follow-up coaching. Otherwise, they are a waste of money and time.

18

Three Essential Competencies

*You cannot get through a single day without having an impact
on the world around you. What you do makes a difference,
and you have to decide what kind of difference you want to make.*

—JANE GOODALL

Implementation versus execution. Proactive Recovery Plans. Outcome-driven meetings. I seldom see these three essential competencies addressed in typical management-training programs, but without them, breakdowns occur frequently and easily turn into crises.

Implementation versus Execution

"Implementation" and "execution" are often used synonymously, but they're actually quite different: implementation refers to initiating a change, new initiative, or project, while execution refers to *acting on it* afterward. Most breakdowns occur during execution, even after what appears to be effective implementation that includes good communication, project planning, and task management. Analysts at a multiregional medical system, for instance, recognized that sick leave dropped significantly when employees received flu shots, so they instructed each medical center to ensure at least 50 percent of their workforce got one.

One medical center spent considerable time developing their human-resources policy, communicated the "why" for the directive, and mapped out a schedule to implement it within a month. They even provided on-site specialists to give the shots.

Implementation went great. All the directors communicated the agreed-upon message and schedule to their teams. But they didn't *execute* well. Only 10 percent showed up to get the shot. So management decided to implement the policy again, this time with more emphasis on how important it was—which was as effective as a mother calling louder to a teenager focused on a video game.

I faced a comparable situation when my then-wife and I assigned new after-school chores to our daughter to encourage her to take more responsibility at home. My wife and I were perfectly aligned. We "implemented" the new chores with the most positive intention and communication—and our daughter ignored us.

I couldn't blame her. My wife and I had never considered the conflict she would face between her chores, homework, and studying for tests, so we never created any exceptions for her school obligations—or consequences for not doing what we wanted her to do when we wanted her to do it. In fact, we never talked about timing issues at all—did we expect her to do the dishes immediately after a meal, or could she wait until the next day to run the dishwasher?

As a result, our daughter did not clearly understand what my wife and I expected from her, nor how she could possibly accomplish it while also fulfilling her school obligations. We'd never sat down together and hammered out an agreement that made sense for all of us.

The medical center had the same execution problem. Senior management never considered that some people get sick from flu shots and so would be unable to perform certain duties or effectively respond to patients afterward, possibly for days. Those who did home health care or worked in field clinics didn't know how to coordinate coming to the hospital building just to get a shot: "Which patient should I put off for this? And what should I do afterwards—go back to work? Or go home and recover?" And, of course, some people refused the shot for cultural or religious reasons.

Since the medical center's target was 50 percent, it needed to set execution boundaries and consequences for those people who could, but didn't, get their flu shot. To stop the senior management team before they reimplemented their policy yet again, I said, "Hang on. Let's identify the circumstances and challenges of execution after implementation."

It only took them about fifteen minutes to identify the problems and brainstorm a strategy and recovery plan.

- Flu shots will be given toward end of the workday, so if people have a reaction, they can go home, rest, and take care of themselves.

- People in the field will get their flu shot right after their usual weekly meeting at the hospital, or they can bring in a note from their local pharmacy confirming they'd received it elsewhere.

- People who don't want the shot for religious or health reasons are exempted.

- Anyone not exempted who doesn't get their flu shot within a month will be counseled on its benefits, at which time any concerns will be addressed.

They also set up a fun, inspirational contest and hung thermometer posters to track their progress. By the end of the next month, 40 percent of the medical center's employees had gotten their flu shot by the end of the season—while short of their target, it was a major improvement.

Proactive Recovery Plans

There are things that we can all do to build resilience in ourselves, but also to build resilience in each other.

—Sheryl Sandberg

The highest-performing organizations recover quickly when breakdowns occur because they already have their Proactive Recovery Plans in place.

Back when I was a beginner skier, I took a lesson from Dave, a US Olympic ski team coach and one of Mt. Bachelor's top instructors in Bend, Oregon. I began by losing my balance as I got off the ski lift. Super embarrassed at how ridiculous I looked trying to stay on my feet and skis, I apologized to Dave.

He responded, "That was outstanding!"

"Yeah, right . . . real graceful!"

"No, not graceful," he admitted, "but what an excellent recovery! Recovery is key for skiers—you must learn to fall properly and recover when you get off balance. Recovery is the secret skill that lets excellent skiers take the most risks!"

The best athletes, musicians, and actors know they won't perform perfectly every time, so they spend hours practicing and rehearsing to develop "Proactive Recovery Plans" for every kind of breakdown, whether it's theirs, someone else's, the equipment's, or even the result of unforeseen circumstances. After all, strings break in the middle of violin performances. Balls take unexpectedly bad hops on the field. And customers cancel orders out of the blue due to their own internal issues. The "human factor" is a constant element of high performance. Everyone has off days or goofs now and then. Everyone inadvertently misjudges situations and neglects to anticipate what might go wrong. But professionals always respond in a prepared, predetermined manner when the unexpected happens.

A string broke on the concert violinist's instrument during a symphony one of our team members attended in Chile. As the orchestra continued to play, he placed his violin on his lap and stretched out his hands. The player next to him put his own violin in the man's hands, replaced and tuned the broken string, played the instrument for a while to warm it up, and then exchanged it back to the concert violinist. The whole maneuver took about ninety seconds and was so smooth and quick, most of the audience probably never saw it.

Can you imagine them making that double switch if they had not practiced it to perfection?

Yet we expect perfection-without-practice in business. We paralyze our forward motion by refusing to admit mistakes will happen. No one can "plan on" perfection. That just creates an unsafe risk-avoidance environment wherein it's not safe to make mistakes. All change comes with a learning curve, though, during which people *will* make mistakes!

"We demand perfection to ensure customer satisfaction and employee safety," managers constantly tell me—and yes, that's both critical and true. We always strive to perfect everything we do. But perfection is a goal, not a state of being. High expectations will never prevent breakdowns or stop people from making mistakes. Leaders who recognize that reality also understand they must have *prepared, practiced responses* for those small breakdowns to keep them from becoming safety or customer-service issues—just as the Tesla staff had its Proactive Recovery Plan when my new car needed immediate repair. Yes, there was a problem, but my inconvenience as a customer was minor, and I left with a good feeling about how the dealership took care of me.

Proactive Recovery Plans are not the same thing as "risk-mitigation" or "contingency" plans, which address flawed decisions and technical breakdowns. That type of planning rarely, if ever, considers such "human" errors as communication breakdowns, unkept commitments, or even simple mistakes.

Tom's IS organization knew its Proactive Recovery Plans were a key core competence when it raised its delivery and satisfaction rate from 25 percent to 75 percent on all projects and to 100 percent on the ten priority projects. Even though the team previously made risk-mitigation plans, their project teams' recovery plans were reviewed in every meeting, just like a professional athletic team or music group—and they involved all impacted parties to ensure each functional area's recovery plan coordinated with all the other areas' plans.

Proactive Recovery in Action

A midwestern medical center had already implemented several B State changes and understood the value of Proactive Recovery Plans when they moved two nursing units from the second to the fourth floor to reduce operating expenses.

This was not a popular change—all the nurses were disgruntled—but the two units worked together to make it happen. They mapped out patient flow, discussed how the supplies in each unit would be organized, determined how to move the second floor's equipment, and developed a Proactive Recovery Plan in case things didn't happen as planned. They also got senior management and other cross-functional departments to guarantee quick response and approval to any new proposals or changes.

Both nursing units moved at the same time—one move worked, the other didn't. The second unit had a major problem that increased patient wait times and complaints, but the nursing staff, albeit unhappy about these new issues, never complained. Instead, they got together with their supervisors and proposed a temporary return to the second floor so they could solve the patient-service breakdowns and then replan their move.

Senior management quickly reviewed and approved their proposal as promised. All the cross-functional departments helped them move back to the second floor. Once patient satisfaction returned to its usual high level, the nurses created a new plan, sent the proposal to senior management, got it approved, and returned—once again with the help of all cross-functional departments—to the fourth floor.

This time, the change was successful.

"How much time do you suppose it took from beginning to end?" I usually ask other medical-center leaders. "They moved to the fourth floor, discovered there was a problem, created a plan to move back, got senior management approval, made the move, rectified the patient-flow issues, replanned the move, got approval again, and then actually moved to the fourth floor permanently."

"Six months to a year?" is the usual response.

"Nope! They did it all in thirty days. And, as a result of all parties' effective cooperation and multiple-change executions, morale went way up in the entire organization."

Proactive Recovery Plans Build Trust and Reduce Stress

Organizations may implement core-values, team-building, and trust-training programs to improve their cultural trust and support, but relationships, trust, and support are honed in the fire of stressful times, when people need to respond quickly and think on their feet. Trust is founded on knowing we can count on everyone involved to complete specific actions in a challenging situation. That's why military, fire, and police units constantly practice their response to emergency situations—and why having a Proactive Recovery Plan is just as important in our personal life for when plans don't work out or something beyond our control happens.

My wife and I have different approaches to resolving our conflicts. I think globally, then locally; she thinks locally, then globally. The big picture leaves her confused and unfocused if she doesn't have the details; I need the big picture, or the details overwhelm me. She needs time alone to process a disagreement; I need to talk about it and move to resolution as quickly as possible.

After a few breakdowns that escalated more than necessary, we decided to create a Proactive Recovery Plan that would work for both of us. When my wife is triggered, she says, "I'm feeling crispy." I know that means I need to give her space to sort out the issue for herself. In return, she committed to get "more neutral" within a couple of hours so we can talk again rather than argue the rest of the day. And though we set this up to support *her*, I've learned having space to "get neutral" helps me, too. When we come back together, we each take ownership of what triggered us and share our positive intentions. Then we surface any miscommunications or misunderstandings, so we can learn from the situation and realign. We now have less friction, a stronger bond, and more confidence and trust that we can quickly resolve any misunderstanding with love and learning, thanks to our Proactive Recovery Plan. It lowers the stress when we do disagree, and it eliminates the illusion either of us must be perfect.

People are less patient, more short-tempered, and emotionally vulnerable when they're stressed, tired, or overwhelmed, so Proactive Recovery Plans help couples, families, teams, and organizations navigate those difficult times without creating the trust or support issues that can plague or even fracture otherwise good relationships.

Marcela Valencia, one of our B State senior consultants with the Coaching Group (www.coachinggroup.net) in Bogotá, for example, purchased airline tickets, rented a car, and made resort reservations for her husband, mother, brother, niece, nephew, and herself in Costa Rica. Everyone was excited about this vacation for the whole family! But when they got to the Bogotá airport ticket counter, the agent asked for everyone's proof of vaccination—which one person did not realize they needed. They couldn't get on the plane.

The family reacted as families so often do. The brother got angry and said he was going home. The mother was sad and disengaged from the rest of the family. The husband didn't outwardly react but seemed paralyzed about what to do. But Marcela—who taught proactive recovery planning—thought, *Okay, wow! We've got a new adventure. We can jointly create a new vacation everyone will enjoy—even my brother.* She looked up alternative flights and talked with the ticket agent about rerouting them for the same cost. "Forget it," the sister said. "It's impossible. Airlines never make these kinds of changes." But thirty minutes later, the family had new tickets to Panama, which didn't require vaccinations. Before they took off, Marcela and her husband quickly secured a resort even better than the one in Costa Rica—and everyone loved their adventure vacation together.

B State Meetings

Team is about making each other better.

—Jim Barnes, CEO, enVista supply-chain consulting

The third essential B State competency is the meeting. A State meetings waste time, use up resources, and drain enthusiasm with their topic-driven, presentation-oriented, metric-ridden agendas. We all know the drill:

"I have too many meetings."

"I'm in so many meetings I don't have time to get my projects and tasks completed."

"I spend most meetings listening to presentations or information I already heard in *other* meetings."

"My meetings overlap, so if I'm in one, I'm absent from the other. I feel like I'm always missing an important conversation or decision."

"Our meetings focus on dashboards but provide little help to impact our metrics—they mostly address *who* needs to be more accountable."

B State meetings don't adhere to a topic-stuffed agenda. Instead, they're quick, productive, engaging, useful—and even fun. Accomplishments that indicate success take priority over reviewing metrics, so participants can concentrate on improving Collective Execution. There are no long, eye-crossing PowerPoint presentations. No racing through agenda items. No endless leadership monologues. No infighting between competing managers. No falling into tangential rabbit holes.

In A State meetings, people tune out when they're not directly involved in a particular project or topic. In B State meetings, the uninvolved take on the critical role of objective problem solvers. People come prepared to drive closure on those matters of the greatest priority and impact—there's no room for nonpriority matters, despite their apparent "urgency." B State meetings—

- Surface and solve breakdowns associated with poor handoffs, conflicts, miscommunication, resistance to change, and unforeseen problems.
- Ensure everyone is on track with their previous "Team Habits and Agreements" commitments.
- Create clear, accountable action plans based on "shared ownership" for achieving results.
- Conclude with everyone agreeing to communicate and behave with "one voice"—even to the point of anticipating challenges and reactions, and developing feedback loops to address unexpected questions or issues.

These kinds of meetings are simply the norm in most professional endeavors outside the business world. Even if you're not an athlete, you've probably seen movies where the coach shows the last game's tape, so everyone can review breakdowns and discuss changes before the team takes to the court, field, or diamond to practice for the next game.

Where A State meetings can easily get out of hand when too many people crowd into the room, B State meetings remain focused, interactive, and productive no matter how many dozens of people attend. And while new B State groups may break into smaller problem-solving subgroups who come back together to make final decisions and commitments, over time—as trust, cross-functional knowledge, and communication increase—the team becomes just as skilled operating as a whole.

19

B State Staff Success

When you talk, you are only repeating what you already know.
But if you listen, you may learn something new.

–DALAI LAMA

If the leadership's culture changes, will the staff's culture be altered even if they aren't part of the change process? Yes, it will—except when A State managers get stuck in the old paradigm. Then their staff gets left behind because it isn't safe for them to get more involved in the new culture.

B State Transformation in Government

A municipality needed to break down silos and build cross-functional ownership to improve community service and reduce operating costs necessitated by decreased funding. Only one division's leadership embraced the transformation at first. They used David Rodgers, one of IMPAQ's B State senior consultants, to lead the successful change effort. When the other divisions saw how it had achieved those goals in only six months, a second division's leadership team began their B State process. Together, they saved the municipality millions of dollars by the end of the year, plus immensely improved the working relationship between the two divisions—and, even better, increased their staffs' engagement and support.

Based on their leadership's modeling, employees adopted the language and tools of B State change: They turned to each other to solve problems rather than default to the chain of command. They volunteered for improvement efforts and suggested changes rather than complain—and in response, management listened to them and acted on their ideas. At the second year, the remaining two divisions began their B State change effort—after which, finally, the senior management team did the same.

That's right: middle management made the transformation before senior management. And that's okay, because it all got done!

The SMT chose "improving employee engagement" as a top priority based on the previous year's low assessment scores, and the city manager told the human resources director to lead that project, as usual. About three months later, the HR director called David to discuss their employee-engagement program.

"I'm creating this program because I was directed to," she said, obviously frustrated, "but I don't believe employee engagement is an HR issue. I think it's a leadership issue."

"You're right," David agreed. "Every manager and supervisor needs to create the *safety* and expectation for *meaningful* engagement."

"That's right! A program won't create the necessary safety if the manager hasn't fostered that environment."

"So let's sort out your situation," David offered. "You did the employee-engagement survey more than nine months ago. Can you do another, smaller-scale assessment to see if anything has changed based on the B State culture transformation?"

"That's a good idea," she said. "I've heard there's greater employee engagement, but I don't know if it's widespread or just a few isolated cases."

The small survey revealed the correlation David expected: the further along in implementing their B State transformation the division was, the more employees were engaged by their supervisors. By midyear, the employee-engagement project was replaced by a B State *focus* on employee engagement, and division leaders asked HR to sponsor workshops so *all* staff could develop general leadership skills, including personal accountability, B State delegation, and team accountability.

B State Solution to a Morale and Retention Problem

A public university struggled to attract top talent for their IT department and hold on to those they had. No matter what programs they implemented, they could not move the needle to improve the department's staff relationships, low morale, or high turnover. Employees knew they could double their salary by working for any of a number of local private IT corporations, and jobs were plentiful. I faced a team of fifty managers, supervisors, and IT staff, all clearly faced off in an "us versus them" mentality when I arrived to implement a B State transformation. The initial session wasn't easy with all that skepticism and negativity, but they nevertheless developed a Picture of Success and Team Habits and committed to follow the process and keep their commitments.

I arrived early for the six-month follow-up session to observe the participants enter the room. I wanted to see whether anyone's attitudes or behavior had changed. It looked like nothing had—people were still unfriendly with each other or, pointedly, with me.

Well, this isn't going to be a very fun day, I thought. *I wonder if they had any success at all.*

I had them individually complete the B State Team Relationship Assessment, as always. During their accomplishments brainstorm, I learned they *had* met and worked on their committed improvement efforts, but no one *felt* any sense of achievement. They'd experienced many improvements in teamwork, communication, and project completion—including measurable reductions in cost and advances in quality and internal-customer satisfaction—but I didn't see that the group's relationship "needle" had moved.

We reviewed their Picture of Success and rerated all twenty Team Habits. They did great: 70 percent of their Team Habits improved, 39 percent significantly. Even so, the people in the room had *no* positive energy. They all just stared at me, expressionlessly. Only one Team Habit scored lower than before, which is quite normal. Just as I began to review that habit with the group, a staff member raised her hand.

"I think the 70 percent improvement in our Team Habits is fake!"

"What! How was it fake? You saw the process. We did it right here, in the room, together."

"You and the management team manipulated those results," she shot back.

Most of the IT staff nodded in agreement.

"I'm lost," I admitted. "How do you figure we manipulated anything, since the rating process was visible at all times to everyone in the room?"

"The last time we were together, we rated the Team Habits in the afternoon," she said. "This time, we rated them in the morning. And we all know everyone is more positive in the morning than the afternoon, so of course the scores were higher."

I paused to see whether she was joking—but no. The employees definitely questioned the process. Someone normally comes to my rescue in this kind of situation, but that didn't happen either.

Just silence.

There was no way to win this theoretical debate, so I suggested we look at the correlations from their B State Team Relationship Assessment results—an assessment *always* done first thing in the morning. I'd do the analysis that afternoon, and we'd look at the results together afterward. "Meanwhile," I said, "here are the correlations between Team Habit improvement scores and your average improvement on the fifteen relationship areas." I drew two columns on our flip chart. "These are the norms, so if the ratings were fake, then the correlations couldn't possibly be met."

Team Habits	Relationships
60%	15%
70%	25%
80%	35%

Rather than go back and review the Team Habit that declined, I went on with the follow-up session to set up the priorities and plans for the next six months of improvement.

Sure enough, the review of the B State Team Relationship Assessment clearly showed a correlation between the Team Habit (70 percent) and the Relationship (26 percent).

"According to your list of accomplishments, your elevated Team Habit scores, and your Team Interactions improvements, you've achieved complete alignment," I told the group. "It's statistically impossible to manipulate. So, here's the deal. You can *choose* to either feel good about your accomplishments or keep feeling bad and *make up some story* to validate your negativity. Personally, I accept the scores and your tremendous gains."

Still no reaction—no "we get it" response, or even, "This is great, because it demonstrates what a good team we are." Nothing! Utter silence, as if I were speaking Martian. We only had a half hour left. Then—"Aha! Wait, everyone! We never reviewed the Team Habit that received a lower score! I completely forgot about it. We need to review that before we leave."

Everyone turned to that page in the workbook, and I read the Team Habit aloud. "It's called Positive Attitude and Celebrating Our Wins. We come to work with a positive attitude to contribute to a better work life. We openly celebrate our wins and accomplishments and fully express our appreciation and acknowledgment of others, regardless of position or department area."

I almost burst out laughing. "Are you kidding me? You spent the entire day being negative and denying your clear demonstration of improvement— and the *only* Team Habit that *decreased* was your commitment to positively acknowledge and celebrate your wins! I've gotta ask: Do you suppose there could *possibly* be any correlation between your attitude today and the *only* Team Habit score that went down?"

I wished someone would drop a pin so they could all hear it—everyone in the room was frozen.

"See you in six months!" I said, leaving them all in stunned silence.

Six months later, the group had "miraculously" taken on a completely new energy. People greeted each other as they walked in the room—several individuals even went out of their way to greet me and ask me how I was doing! Friendly laughter and conversation filled the air.

Now, I was the one stunned.

This time, everyone's energy was high as we reviewed their accomplishments. People shouted out wins from all over the room—they wouldn't stop!—and pointedly acknowledged each other's areas. Their Team Habits had improved again, especially the one on "Positive Attitude and Celebrating Our Wins." Afterward, the management team stayed to tell me how grateful they were for my honesty in our last session.

"Everyone took your message to heart."

"Well," I admitted, "you created a happy accident with that unique Team Habit. It spotlighted your negative attitude in a way you couldn't ignore. That's the power of using correlated measurements. The results cannot be denied or manipulated."

The department director called me out of the blue about six years later. "I just want you to know that we're still following your B State system. We've continued to improve every year without exception. Even better, we stopped having a retention problem. We're now attracting the *best* talent in the IT field because they've heard about our culture. Applicants tell us they're willing to take much less compensation to work in a supportive, engaged-team environment that doesn't have the backbiting and cliques found in private industry. Instead of constantly searching for help, we're now turning away people!"

A Call Center Transformation

We've successfully implemented B State changes on every level of every kind of organization. A multinational corporation's regional sales department, for example, constantly complained about their call center's poor customer service—hardly an unusual occurrence. Upper management, blaming lack of commitment and accountability, implemented a new set of goals, metrics, and customer-service training, but employees were overwhelmed and confused by all the changes and pressure to perform. Although Jane Grossman, another IMPAQ B State senior consultant, was called in to "fix the call-center reps," she recognized that the management team needed a B State transformation first.

The management team created a Picture of Success focused on eliminating silos, and then determined the most effective tools and metrics to achieve the highest level of customer-satisfaction. Next, Jane implemented a B State Accountability workshop with the call-center reps. Within one year, the call center received customer-satisfaction scores in the high 8s (out of 10). Not only did they exceed corporate's target goal of 8.0, they were the *only* region that *consistently* achieved it. The sales organization stopped complaining and instead recognized the call-center reps for their consistent responsiveness, which has continued for more than a decade as of this writing.

B State Work-Life Balance

Winning is important to me, but what brings me real joy is the experience of being fully engaged in whatever I'm doing.

—Phil Jackson

Purpose-driven, safe, and supportive environments are *fun*! It's a blast to feel part of a team that works together and enjoys success beyond expectations! Yes, it takes dedication, consistency, and hard work to get those breakthrough results, but as one of my mentors said, "When you do something one hundred percent, it's a breeze. When you do something ninety-five percent, it's a bitch!"

Isn't that the truth? When we put ourselves completely into something, we don't feel the effort or passing time because we're fully present and involved in what we're doing. But when we multitask or become unbalanced, we create a mental conundrum, a bifurcation that creates stress and makes us "feel" how hard we're working—and that's a recipe for misery.

Sometimes, the imbalance isn't work related; it's a home issue. B State employees who learn about developing agreements, Team Habits, and Proactive Recovery Plans with their team members and supervisors often discover those same ideas can remedy issues with their spouses, children, and other family members.

When I used to spend weekends with my eight-year-old daughter after my divorce, work regularly interrupted our time together. "You're always on the phone," she complained—and she was right. I still worked weekends at that point to grow my business and secure her present and future. We agreed that I would give her a minimum of two solid, uninterrupted hours within every six-hour period, and she'd play by herself or read the rest of the time while I worked. Of course, she soon discovered that spending any more than two hours with Dad got boring, so even the breaks worked out well. She immediately pointed out the one time I forgot, and I got right back on track. My show of respect for her and our agreement not only increased the trust between us, but made her feel safe and, by extension, gave her confidence to speak up with other people in similar situations.

I was running a B State Mastership program once when Alan spoke up: "I had the most amazing breakthrough with my family last night. I've been having a lot of problems with my fifteen-year-old son, and my wife keeps telling me, 'You're just not approachable.' So last night, I called a family meeting. I told them about what we did yesterday in our B State training session and admitted I wasn't communicating effectively with them. Then I led us through creating our own family habits around keeping each other informed and making decisions that include my son's input. He was amazing—completely clear and direct about what he needed, yet willing to accommodate my needs as well. My wife was supportive of both of us. It was truly the best conversation we'd had in years. This morning, everyone was in great spirits. We even talked to each other over breakfast instead of snarling, like we usually do."

He looked at me. "Mark, I have to thank you. I've been pretty shut down up to this point, but your tools are so practical, they even work at home. You've changed my life!"

B State Partnerships

In typical partnerships, each party goes into self-protection mode, which generates petty "you versus me" disputes. "I'm doing all the giving; you're just taking." Everyone looks out for themselves, not for the partnership. But in a B State, everyone looks out for both the whole and each other. It eliminates silos, whether they're between a couple, within a family, or in a business environment.

I saw this in action when I worked with a nuclear plant's manager who had high expectations of his workforce yet looked out for his employees' best interests and insisted they take care of themselves. If he noticed someone feeling sick or knew they had a pressing family issue, he sent them home. Not only did his plant have one of the highest employee-satisfaction scores in its field, but its industry regulatory agency rated it the number-one nuclear plant in the country.

That B State advantage even works in independent-contractor organizations, such as my own company, IMPAQ. Our consultants share commissions with each other and the operational staff not because it's required, but because we established that B State cultural norm decades ago. We take care of each other for the good of every person and the organization as a whole.

20

B State Transformation Challenges and Failures

I learned that courage was not the absence of fear, but the triumph over it. The brave man is not he who does not feel afraid, but he who conquers that fear.

—NELSON MANDELA

Some people just do not want to change how they do things, period, no matter how many agreements they sign to be supportive or how many behavior workshops they attend.

I cringe at stories of employees who contribute new ideas, only to have their supervisor ignore or dismiss them rather than risk the hassle of *their* manager's disapproval. It's a vicious circle—employees feel frustrated, disrespected, and overlooked, while upper management feels frustrated about their employees' lack of engagement! No one wants to take that all-important first step forward, so everyone loses.

Why? Because everyone is stuck.

I've seen senior and middle managers get stuck when their recommended improvements were endlessly challenged in analysis paralysis. And, as absurd as it sounds, I've even seen ideas rejected simply because the person who came up with it wasn't part of the "inner circle"—as if they were still in high school!

That's what happened in Bogotá when Eduardo was brought in to transform his sales department from transactional to strategic. Previous new managers had been demonized as ineffective when they tried to improve the organization's effectiveness or profitability, so Eduardo started with a two-month assessment that revealed his team members had no sales goals, training, or management. Based on that indisputable knowledge, he announced his plan to change the sales process, introduce goals, and provide extensive training to everyone to support their success. For a B State organization, that would have been exciting. But for this A State organization, it was threatening—and rejected.

The very night of Eduardo's announcement, three of his most senior team members asked him to dinner. He was thrilled—a perfect opportunity to get to know his top sales managers and talk about their exciting new role! But barely past their first round of drinks, they attacked him. "We're not interested in changing our sales process or roles. We know what you're doing—you've been talking to Paul too much. He may be a senior manager, but nobody likes or trusts him. So, forget it—we're not going along with your ideas."

Feeling he'd been body slammed, Eduardo ate his dinner without further discussion. But the next day, he decided to outflank the three by working with his salespeople one at a time. When he eventually presented the negative "external drivers" and "internal breakdowns" he'd uncovered to his extended-leadership team—which included two of the three people who'd confronted him—and shared a Picture of Success that provided clear direction, most of the group thought he made a lot of sense.

Only those still entrenched in A State resisted getting engaged.

But with the majority's support, Eduardo started training sessions. He created teams out of salespeople whose products could (and should) be presented as part of a package, rather than as individual items. As expected, the department's largest key accounts responded favorably to this more strategic/consultative approach. This simple yet effective change, which should have taken a matter of months, took over a year to fully implement due to resistance, but ultimately, even the three naysayers got on board and supported the transformation.

B State Failures

Our six- and twelve-month assessments conducted over twenty years prove the B State transformation is successful 95 percent of the time. That 5 percent failure is usually due to either one individual's ego, or the team's lack of follow-through.

People in his organization thought of "Dave" as an expert, even a hero, due to his critical-thinking abilities and problem-solving competence. On the other hand, they also thought he micromanaged, and that while sometimes his input added clarity, mostly it was stifling or confusing, especially when he gave orders to people below his direct reports—or when he delegated a project to two different direct reports without letting either one know about the other. He constantly undermined whatever B State transformation his team tried to implement with his adamant refusal to change. Obviously, his team was part of the 5 percent "fail" statistic.

Another senior leadership team's B State efforts were disrupted by one team member's need to be right. He yelled and blamed others whenever someone introduced any solution other than his. I once saw him so out of control during a meeting that the team leader told him to leave the room. Fortunately, he didn't prevent his team's successful B State transformation, but we had to include frequent follow-ups in their B State Team Agreements to keep them on track.

Timing Is Everything

In yet another organization, the department manager's need to be liked and accepted by her direct reports kept her from ever setting clear expectations or holding her team members accountable, even when the division leader put her department on probation. Her team members didn't think they needed to change, and she couldn't figure out how to hold them accountable.

They brought us in to do a B State transformation, but at the six-month follow-up visit to measure their results in Collective Execution, Project Deliverables, and Team Relationships, they didn't meet our standard improvement norms. "Clearly," I told them, "you didn't keep your commitments or follow the system we agreed on six months ago. There's no point wasting your time or mine if you aren't committed to the process."

Consultants don't do that. They were obviously all shocked—their body language closed down—but no one dared say a word. So I went on.

"Your department is failing based on your division leader's expectations, which was the whole point of this investment six months ago. So, you have a choice: Either recommit to this B State transformation, or let's cancel the rest of our session together and call it a day. We can all go back to our jobs. Your call. I'll step outside so you can talk amongst yourselves and make a decision."

"Wait a minute!" one team member shouted. "Why didn't you tell us six months ago that the division leader thinks we're failing?"

"Excuse me?" the director piped up. "We not only discussed that at the beginning of the session six months ago, we've talked about this in a lot of other meetings since then."

"Yeah, okay," another team member said. "But we all thought this was just another team-building exercise like all the others that never meant a thing after we completed it."

"Besides," someone else said, "how do we know your method is the right one for us?"

"Maybe it isn't," I admitted. "But you might ask yourselves what method *will* work for you when you already set your own direction and came to agreements with each other, but then didn't bother to follow through? We don't have time to debate what happened six months ago—and we don't need to find blame. Your only assignment now is to decide amongst yourselves whether or not you will commit to this process. If yes, then when I come back you'll have to clarify the specific attitudes and behaviors you *will* exhibit going forward to demonstrate your commitment, and we'll continue getting your team back on track for the rest of the day. Otherwise . . ."

I left the room.

They took a full hour before they called me back into the room.

"We agreed," one team member stated for the rest. "We'll do your B State process."

"Fine," I said. "So, what will you do differently?"

"We'll follow through and keep our commitments."

"If we don't think we can keep a commitment," someone else said, "we'll say so in the meeting rather than agree and not do it later."

"Good," I said. "I expect to see you all exhibit those behaviors in the time we have left as we develop new commitments and agreements." I turned to the director. "And what will *you* do differently in the next six months as the leader of this team?"

"That was part of our discussion when you were out of the room," she admitted. "I've agreed to be a stronger leader from now on and hold people accountable, both individually and as a team. We're *all* going to treat this session as critical. We *all* need to do things differently—and we're open to change and look forward to actively implementing this process."

"Good!" I responded. "It *is* serious—some of your jobs will depend on it—so let's get started. We don't have much time."

We didn't have to re-create what they did previously—that had been pretty good. We just focused on implementation and execution and gave more attention to their recovery plans, since they had a lot of conflicting priorities with the corporate office.

"You look like a different team," I said at the end of the day.

"This was so much better than our first session together," admitted one team member.

"Yeah, it's a different experience when you're fully engaged and committed."

"No, it really was different," someone else said. "There was more energy, and it was so much more fun this time!"

I didn't say, "That's because you actually paid attention and didn't just shine me on." Instead, I merely said, "I'm glad you made the choice to recommit. I'll be back to remeasure your results in three months. I expect you to deliver on *all* of your six-month-old commitments, so you'd better stay as dedicated and supportive of each other as you are right now!"

"We can do it!" the director chimed in, grinning.

Three months later, everyone was ecstatic. They'd made up for all their lost time, and their measurements did indeed indicate a huge success. They'd even gotten positive feedback from other departments.

"We're not the same team we were when you first started working with us," one person assured me. "We show up differently with each other and to our internal customers."

"People have so much more respect for us now," another said. "Others even seek *us* out for advice—that's *never* happened before."

"They really did make a lot of progress," the division leader told me. "It just took them too long. I'd already decided to replace the director with someone else."

That's not uncommon: when leaders don't produce results fast enough, they get replaced—often, right after they finally make a breakthrough. This was a big win for the team, but an unfortunate temporary "fail" for their leader. Having learned how to effectively set expectations and hold her team accountable, she went on to become a more successful leader in another organization.

Leader Sabotage

Everybody was pumped at a large trucking company after the team developed their Picture of Success and new Team Habits. Several people told me on the final break how practical and positive the process was for addressing their challenges. But at the end of the day, the division vice president, who was part of the team, said, "This was a nice exercise, but I'm the one who will set this team's Picture of Success and new Team Habits."

My jaw dropped. "But . . . you were part of this process! We talked about how this all works together, just you and me, weeks ago. Is there something in what the team developed you don't agree with?"

"Nope! But I'm the boss. We won't be continuing this process. Thanks for coming in."

His team members were as shocked as I was—but he was the boss. No one said anything. They just returned to their jobs, their enthusiasm dashed, their engagement shattered. Definitely one of our 5 percent failures.

Middle-Management Power Struggles

B State transformations that unify upper-middle managers are the fastest way to break down silos, accelerate the pace of change, and transform functional managers into business leaders. As if they get an instant leadership promotion, team members gain greater influence with senior management, develop more authority in the organization, and become change agents to improve cultural norms.

Yet I've seen middle-management power struggles arise during B State implementations that never surface in senior management, department, or project teams.

I was asked to help a twenty-five-member middle-management group become a unified team. Flanked by three members of the senior leadership team, their CEO, Carla, kicked off the session.

"Our organization is experiencing several challenges," she announced, "and we believe your leadership as a unified team can help move us forward. Mark already implemented a B State Leadership Accountability System with our senior leadership team—it really helped us align and improve our teamwork. We've brought him back to help you in the same way. We look forward to your output at the end of the session."

The other senior leaders then validated the CEO's message with personal notes on how much they had learned and benefited from the process while the middle managers listened attentively.

"We'll leave you now," Carla wrapped up, "and let you have your time with Mark. But if you have any questions, please feel free to contact any of us during the next two days."

Everything went fine until after the initial B State concepts had been shared and the team began developing their Picture of Success.

That's when the power struggles surfaced.

In one subgroup, three managers dominated the discussion and refused to listen to their teammates. Bob, one of the disregarded, said, "I'm not sure we've put in enough detail to make this a strong statement. It sounds too generic."

"This statement is great as it is," replied Julie, the leader of the three dominators. "I've done this kind of exercise before. This is a perfect statement."

But when I came over and tested it using the 1 to 5 numbering system, the statement failed. It didn't indicate a big enough transformation.

"I'm sorry," I said, "but you need to work on your statement to make it more of a stretch."

"You weren't clear on your number system," Julie countered, "because this is very well written and represents a stretch."

"Okay," I said. "Let me explain the system again before you give your rating, to make sure it's well understood."

After my explanation, Julie said, "See? You weren't clear, so of course it didn't pass the test."

We tested the statement again—it failed again. So I shared a couple of ways the team could improve their paragraph to make it a clearer stretch, but by then Julie and her two cohorts were sending me angry looks. The rest of the subgroup looked at each other and stayed quiet.

Once each of the subgroups passed the test and the larger group modified each of the three statements, I read them all together, as usual. But unlike most groups, this one didn't feel proud of their Picture of Success. It was silent. People looked at each other to see whether it was okay to praise what they'd accomplished.

Clearly, these middle managers were divided between an "in group" and . . . everyone else. Most of the new team members—the ones who contributed great clarity to their paragraphs—were part of the "everyone else."

The in-group clique consisted of all "old timers" whose arrogance had grown over the years to the point they were now obstinate around anyone who challenged their powerful influence. Some were individual high performers with strong silos—others were just good at hiding their nonperformance.

Working with this group and its prevailing negativity the next day was like pulling teeth. "Is everything okay?" I asked the group as we continued to develop Team Habits, ratings, and committed areas for improvement. "Does anyone want to raise an issue or concern?"

Silence, punctuated by wary glance exchanges.

"Everything's fine," Julie proclaimed. "Let's keep going."

Even though the room felt negative, we completed the day, the group did great work, and everyone gained a lot of clarity and commitment to their plans for improvement—and the CEO and senior leaders were very impressed.

The following week, Bill, the vice president of human resources, called. "After the first day of your session," he said, "several middle managers got together to reject your authority. They criticized your style, your passive-aggressive behavior, and some of the personal stories you shared. They said you lost all credibility with them."

"That's interesting," I answered, "because when I asked if they had any issues, all I got was silence. I'm sorry if I upset anyone. I take ownership for everything I said during the session and will apologize if you think it's necessary."

"I don't think you need to do anything at this point," he said. "We habitually get this kind of attitude from some of our middle managers."

"That's too bad. If it's a prevailing attitude, that means their individual senior leader is allowing it. This is where you as senior leaders need to take a stronger stance to set norms of behavior and attitude."

"Yes," Bill admitted. "That's a weakness of ours. We're starting to address it."

The group had clearly made huge improvements by the six-month Evaluation Session. But as we reviewed the scores that demonstrated those great gains, Julie broke in with, "We didn't make these improvements because of your system. We were on track to make these improvements anyway."

"That's not how I see it," a newer team member countered. "We had several breakdowns in our coordination, information sharing, and communications that have improved in the past six months from our efforts in this process. I've been here for two years, and this is the first time I can get things done without unnecessary disruptions."

"Honestly, it doesn't matter how you made those improvements," I said. "I'm just surprised you aren't celebrating your higher scores and accomplishments! It's your success, no matter how you achieved it."

Again, I was met with silence. Some people looked angry or shut down.

"I feel like I'm the enemy here," I continued, "which is odd to me, because my only purpose is to help you to gain influence as leaders of this organization. I promoted your good work to senior leadership. I'm here as your advocate and support system. I gave you a voice where you didn't have one before, to make changes you want to make. Yet I feel attacked. I don't get it."

I sat in front of the group and waited. Finally, Barbara, one of the quieter members of part of the in-group, spoke up. "We did get benefit, and we want to continue this process of making improvements. But we want to do it our own way instead of your way."

"Okay, great!" I responded. "How do you want to go forward?"

"We want to choose new areas for improvement and get into new groups using our own process."

"Fantastic! This is your team, and how you work the process is in your own hands. I totally support you—provided you continue to get results."

More team members were supportive of the process, as long as they got to do things "their way," yet, somehow, the group still gave off a negative vibe. Nevertheless, six months later, their numbers again demonstrated great improvement.

Over the next year, one of the negative team members was let go, a few others left the organization, and the senior leader who didn't hold anyone accountable for their negative attitude and behavior was replaced. And while this is just one specific example, I've seen a similar pattern with other middle-management groups that have implemented a B State transformation. It always feels as if I'm back in high school, where people protect each other, form cliques, defy authority, and overexert their influence on others for power and control.

Middle managers that have this initial negative attitude and can't let go still achieve vast improvements like the example above. They eventually reach a plateau and become stuck. But I've also witnessed middle managers who started off negative and cynical but were willing to receive feedback and let go of their negativity. They became some of the greatest leaders and change agents I've seen, similar to the Middle-Management Miracle. They are the most grateful for the transformation because they have a visceral memory of their previous unsafe culture.

Unfortunately, this kind of negativity doesn't typically surface or get resolved in normal meetings, management-development courses, or even fun team-building off-sites.

Success, Then Failure

Surprisingly, some organizations fail *after* they achieve significant positive results from their B State transformation. A utility company's director was completely aligned with his team's B State Picture of Success and Team Habits of Collective Execution, and his project managers' projects were finally on track. "For the very first time," one of them told me, "we're surfacing and resolving problems in our meetings instead of just wasting time with updates." Their measured results were significant: Collective Execution, Project Deliverables, and Team Relationships all improved according to plan.

A month later, however, I got a call from a group of those project managers. Their director had replaced the new, effective B State meeting structure with their old, socializing, relationship-focused get-togethers, and they needed advice on how to proceed.

"The only way I might be able to help is to talk with the director," I said.

"Go ahead—and let us know."

"I agree with you," I told the director when I got him on the phone. "Socialization is important. But can't you achieve it in a different way without stopping the meetings that have gotten you such good results?"

"Oh, we'd have gotten those results anyway," he said blithely. "I've made my decision."

I received several more calls from project managers frustrated by increasingly prevalent, unresolved conflicts and swiftly eroding trust. I understood completely. Once people get a taste of operating in a B State, they get even more discouraged when it goes back to A State. I felt terrible for them, but I couldn't help them. The boss was the boss.

Misplaced Loyalty

As CEO, Ben in Canada had a clear vision for his organization and constantly reinforced his commitment to its Picture of Success. He regularly detailed how his multimillion-dollar business and culture needed to change. But his power-hungry, change-phobic, controlling VP of sales, Jerry, who insisted he had to "save the organization" from Ben, constantly told his direct reports to *resist* the CEO's changes—even though the company had enjoyed a number of successes due to the B State transformation.

Once in a while, Jerry appeared to change his mind and get on board with the B State change, but it was always short lived. He'd immediately return to his resistant, silo behavior that undermined cross-functional teamwork. And because Ben considered Jerry one of the smartest and most respected leaders in his organization, he'd confront Jerry about his behavior and actions, but not to the point that he'd risk losing Jerry's knowledge—or the loyalty of Jerry's sales team. Other VPs who had been excited about Ben's Picture of Success eventually questioned his commitment and—afraid of Jerry's retaliation—simply stopped moving toward it. Chalk up another "fail."

Throwing Success Down the Toilet

A poorly rated utility was put on notice: if it didn't improve performance and morale, its national regulatory agency would shut it down. One year after leadership implemented a B State transformation, the company's scores were high enough to be out of danger—one of the fastest and biggest changes the agency had ever witnessed. Its reputation was completely restored. Impressed, the agency hired us to help *them* implement a B State transformation.

But the utility's CEO then decided that since his organization had achieved such miraculous recovery and success, it no longer needed the B State process! He replaced us with a consultant who focused on team building to drive the following year's improvement efforts. To no one's surprise (except the CEO), performance declined to the point that the regulatory agency made good on its promise. The agency's temporary shutdowns eventually led to the plant's permanent closure.

Why did he do it?

While the CEO's decision seems illogical, he simply fell prey to an extremely common human weakness: once he achieved what he wanted, he reverted to his comfort zone. Like a dieter who drops ten pounds on a healthy food regimen, but then returns to old eating habits and gains them all back, he never fully engaged or committed to the Picture of Success or Team Habits that produced his success. He put his own wants and needs above the good of everyone and everything else. That's the same thing outspoken New York Yankees coach Billy Martin did when he decided to take his equally outspoken star player, Reggie Jackson, down a peg.

Jackson usually batted fourth so his home runs would clean up all the runners on base as well. Jackson's anger after Martin moved him to fifth position affected his performance—and the Yankees dropped down to third place. Only after two other ballplayers found the courage to confront Martin did he finally opt to put the team's needs above his own ego. He switched Jackson back to hitting fourth, the Yankees shot back to first place, and Jackson went on to hit three home runs in one game to clinch the World Series.

Sometimes, a recovery plan is as simple as having team members challenge the status quo or the boss's intractable stance. Of course, that means the leaders must listen and accept the good of the team above their own wants and needs.

21

The New Frontier: Partnerships between Companies

Let both sides explore what problems unite us
instead of belaboring those problems which divide us.

–JOHN F. KENNEDY

Organizations merge, acquire each other, and partner with ever-increasing frequency in today's global-oriented marketplace, but over 50 percent of those company combos fail to produce the kind of success their leaders originally envisioned. The weaker of two organizations, fearing the stronger party will dominate them, becomes passive-aggressive. The more successful organization's numbers look bad in light of their new partner's poor ones. Or the larger organization takes control over everything even though their operational systems are not as efficient or productive as the smaller, more agile organization's processes.

Remember Tom, the multinational manufacturing company CIO from chapter 1? One of his key vendors habitually kept his organization in the dark about breakdowns. He figured a stronger partnership was the best solution.

Tom's organization operated with B State efficiency, leaving the vendor clearly perceived as the weaker organization. To avoid what seemed an inevitable failure, Tom paid us to implement a B State transformation with the vendor's leadership team, so they got stronger before the two companies formed their partnership. Although reluctant, the vendor's CEO agreed to let his senior management team work with us—he couldn't really refuse since Tom paid for our services. But neither he nor the company really understood—or wanted—the kind of changes we bring to the table.

The leadership team was willing, but I'd never worked with such a skeptical team before—or had to do a transformation when no one in the organization knew why we were there! Getting their participation was like pulling teeth that first morning, even though we only focused on improving their team and organization. They had no idea what I tried to get across to them. At lunch, the CEO asked, "When will we start discussing the needs of Tom's company?"

I grinned. "Never! We're implementing this process strictly to benefit your organization, not his."

"That makes no sense at all! Why would *he* pay for us to improve *our* company?"

"Because if your execution improves as much as theirs did, you'll not only be a much better supplier, you'll be better positioned to become a true business partner. That's why this effort is completely focused on you."

He said, "Okay," but he and his team did not really accept that we had no ulterior motive until the end of the day, when we were in the middle of creating Team Habits.

"I have to admit," one team member said, "this has been super helpful so far to get us aligned and clarify what we need to do differently as a leadership team."

"This has been an outstanding day," another one admitted. "Definitely something we never experienced before."

"Honestly, I thought you were spies sent to uncover our ineffectiveness and report back to Tom," a third manager said. "I didn't think we could trust you at all—and I certainly didn't believe it when you said everything was confidential! But now that I see the process more fully, I can see your intentions are only to help us be better. And hey, we *all* appreciate that."

"This definitely explains all the improvements we've seen in Tom's leadership team these past few months," another person said.

Everyone participated without hesitation the second day, and their deliverables, Collective Execution, and Team Relationships all improved significantly over the next three months. It was a totally different team than the one I first met. Everyone was much more open, engaged, and clear on their priorities.

Tom got the two leadership teams together to replace their existing customer-supplier relationship with a B State agreement for how they would work together for their mutual benefit. They started by sharing business goals and openly discussing challenges and constraints. No longer concerned that Tom's organization was there to spy out their weaknesses, the vendor's people now voluntarily shared them. Now that the supplier was more open and less conflicted within itself, management could be more courageous and open with their customer. The combined teams' Partnership Picture of Success and Team Habits of Collective Execution included the following:

1. Each partner will help the other achieve their independent company's goals and outcomes, including financial performance expectations.

2. Each partner will help the other develop and train their employees in the technical and project-management competencies missing in their partner organization.

3. Each partner will openly surface problems within their own organization about performance agreements to facilitate joint problem-solving rather than isolated problem-solving.

4. Each partner will hold the other accountable for commitments and agreements without blame and with complete support for making improvements.

5. Proactive Recovery Plans will be developed in joint project planning efforts to provide a clear road map for addressing unexpected breakdowns or changes.

The two leadership teams came together again six months later to evaluate their effectiveness. Although not yet perfect, their execution and performance indicators had clearly improved, and both companies were a lot closer to achieving their financial targets. If the economy had not taken its debilitating downturn in 2008, Tom would have rolled out this new business B State Partnership model with other suppliers on an extensive level, but by the time the economy recovered, Tom had moved up the ladder to a completely different part of the organization.

Two Organizations and a Purchasing Department

The CEO of a worldwide logistics organization felt stuck. He couldn't update his field divisions with the newest communication technologies fast enough to serve customer needs, and the array of stakeholders involved—purchasing, legal, suppliers, and finance, to name a few—complicated the challenge. The new systems had to seamlessly integrate with legacy technology, but the traditional bid-design-deliver approach couldn't keep pace with technological changes. He needed a more competitive cost structure and an open-source bid-design-deliver architecture that unlocked contracts to large and small groups alike. The transition required a new mind-set, new behaviors, and a new business model for the primary suppliers.

One trusted supplier caught the CEO's vision and made a groundbreaking proposal to open their design and delivery practice to others. No one had ever tried this before—it was a huge risk for all involved—but the proposal was accepted. Both CEOs knew they had to move from a customer-supplier relationship to a partnership in mind-set, behavior, and practices or they'd be doomed to failure.

The supplier CEO brought all his functional leaders together to share the purpose and risks of failure involved with the new business model and partnering relationship. They identified all the typical behaviors that *wouldn't* work in this new partnership and prioritized them for aligned and immediate change. They then developed Team Habits to clarify new expectations for internal collaboration and partnership with the logistics company, and created B State Team Agreements to surface breakdowns and support each other when anyone reverted back to old habits. The leaders quickly implemented their changes to prepare for full integration with the logistics organization.

Operations, purchasing, quality, and legal functional leaders from both companies came together for a B State transformation. After developing their Picture of Success and Team Habits to transform their processes and behaviors, everyone clearly understood their new role expectations. They also identified specific process changes between the field and purchasing to become more responsive. In a major shift for the purchasing and legal departments, they committed to develop new, timely decision-making processes with due diligence as they worked in parallel to keep things moving.

The primary supplier identified specific request-receipt parameters and provided an attractive costing structure for quicker purchasing decisions. Every party had to change their approach to each other. The Team Habits were so critical, they were written into the contract between the two organizations. Six months after implementation, three different leaders drafted a statement about the transformation's success, which read:

"The new level of teamwork between all functions and the two companies is palpable. They have successfully implemented the new processes and behaviors to lower costs and speed up decision-making so the field gets their new communication technology to serve their customers."

One of the leaders asked us to assist him with a similar project with another organization.

Transforming a National Health-Care System

Health care's rising costs are a global crisis, for which no country has yet devised a proven solution—especially since expanded life expectancy continually increases those costs. It costs at least five times as much to serve people sixty-five years and older than people in their twenties.

In one country, we led leaders from eight different organizational entities through a B State transformation to improve service and reduce costs. Included were representatives from two major hospitals (each with more than three thousand employees), community-care facilities, mental illness organizations, children's hospitals and care facilities, social care enterprises, and members of the commissioning organization and project-management office associated with transformation.

Their purpose was to improve population-care quality for multiple community sectors, significantly reduce costs, and become a model to resolve the financial crisis. Beyond the partnerships we supported, the transformation also involved several entities with multiple funding streams. They also wanted to remove duplication and improve systems to ensure the simplest, streamlined processes to deliver evidence-based care within and between organizational entities. They identified different population sectors' needs, including the elderly, children, the financially disadvantaged, the financially advantaged, and the mentally/emotionally challenged, to determine the most optimal programs for preventive, ambulatory, and hospital care within subcommunities.

The Transformation Leadership Team (TLT) comprised thirty senior managers, middle managers, physicians, government commissioners, community representatives, and board members. After developing their Picture of Success and fifteen Team Habits for Collective Execution across all entities, they prioritized six initiatives to be accomplished through individual leadership and shared ownership.

Six months later, everyone was animated and motivated. They had built a new level of collaboration between entities, developed a synergy between leaders, and removed obstacles plaguing them all. It was the ultimate B State transformation—everybody won, nobody lost, and the future for this hampered health-care system looked the brightest it had ever been!

No one is ever left "stuck" in a B State.

Epilogue

Companies, families, and individuals constantly want to improve. But with the explosive speed of change happening in our society, our various communities, and around the world, sometimes we cannot afford to simply "improve" or "change." We need to immediately transform who we are, what we're doing, and how we're doing it—just to keep up.

Otherwise, we get left behind—and then no amount of effort, money, or regret can ever regain that lost time and distance.

B State transformation achieves rapid breakthrough results. B State mind-sets, habits, and behaviors are so different they create a new reality—one that does not allow us to simply lapse back to our old state.

But beware: B State transformations are not one-time events. They may last for years, but in all likelihood, at some point we'll need to do another, once again, just to keep up with our evolving dreams, aspirations, and environment.

Acknowledgments

There are so many people who have been loving, supportive, and helpful during the creation of this book that it would be hard to mention them all . . . but I will give it my best try!

I want to thank my family and extended family for all of their continued loving support. My wife, Kamin, is my "rock" and loving support system. I'm also grateful that I've always been surrounded by loving family, including my mom, Meta Samuel, Dad, Michael Samuel, and daughters Sarah Samuel and Leah Miller. I have so much gratitude and respect for Sophie Chiche and Nancy Grossman-Samuel, and several cousins and close friends, including Davee Gunn, Virginia Burt, Paul and Sandi Caplan, Barbara and Stephen State, Marvin and Reinette Levine, Alcene and Bob Looper, Paul and Cindy Henry, Janet and Lawrence Caminite, Chip and Kerry Clitheroe, Polly Clitheroe, Laura Hillman, Robert and Margot Hillman, Dr. Marion and Robert Bell, Martine and Claude Chiche, Sherry and Ivan Grossman, Richard and Phyllis Mitz, Mike and Carol Heiser, Elaine Heiser, Mark and Grace Hennings, Allee Willis, Prudence Fenton, and Kent and Linda Falk.

I especially want to thank Claudia Suzanne for her brilliant and steady coaching and co-writing. She challenged my old writing paradigms to make this my most leading-edge book to date.

I also so appreciate Steve Chandler for his guidance and support, in addition to the foreword he wrote for *B State*. As an authority on accountability, he represents the integrity, attunement, and coaching that fosters some of the best coaches I have ever met.

Thanks to my publicist, Sarah Wilson, and the Greenleaf team who supported and advised me throughout the publishing process, including Tanya Hall, Justin Branch, Tyler LeBleu, Sam Alexander, Jessica Choi, Rachael Brandenburg, Karen Cakebread, Corrin Foster, Chelsea Richards, Steve Elizalde, and Jonathan Hierholzer.

My B State Team at IMPAQ guided me, contributed to the models and thinking behind B State, and supported me for decades. I owe so much to them for their support and inspiration, especially to Annie Hyman Pratt, my business partner, and David Rodgers, my co-leader of IMPAQ. I also have the best team ever, including Jane Grossman, Sharon Rich, Thomas Hempelmann, Anthony Escamilla, Barbara Schindler, Heather McGonigal, Marcos Cajina, Marianne Kruse, Deanna "Drai" Turner, and Lei Lani Fera.

I would like to thank our partners in Bogotá, Colombia, the Coaching Group, including Eduardo Lleras, Marcela Valencia, Ana Cecillia Guingue, Fernando (Nano) Escalon, Luis Manuel Ramirez, and Nathalie Lievano Bahamon.

And many thanks to our partners in Amsterdam, Netherlands, Rainmen Group, including Edo Noppert, Marco Scheele, Robert Nieuwland, Catherine Clercx, Toon van Kleef, Geert Stradmeijer, Auke Veenstra, Ger de Kok, and Jeroen van der Valk.

There are also those individuals who directly pushed me to think outside the box, including Sinan Kanatsiz, Chris Alexandre, Newton Margulies, Marty Brotman, Sylvia Novak, John Morton, Russell Bishop, Ron and Mary Hulnick, Gay and Katie Hendricks, J-R, David Covey, Stephan Mardyks, Mrs. Reidy (sixth grade teacher), and Robert "Bob" Newcomb. I am grateful for the works of Esther Hicks-Abraham, Wayne Dyer, and Marianne Williamson. You always encouraged me to stretch myself and go beyond my limitations and boundaries.

As a partial history of my evolution in developing Accountable Organizations and now B State Transformation, I would like to thank the many people who contributed to my thinking along the way, including Todd

Alexander, Allan Matos, J. D. Bowles, Jonathan Ellerby, David Bransky, Leslie Smith, Geri Lopker, David Covey, Nancy Brown-Johnston, Joerg Schmitz, Michael Nila, Frank Brillman, Valerie Lew-Kiedrowski, Sue and Ken Bingham, Teresa Roche, Barbara Thrasher, Cynthia David, Jonathan Wygant, Patrick Carmichael, Licia Rester-Frazee, Dr. Newton Margulies, Drs. Ron and Mary Hulnick, Michael Murphy, John Morton and Leigh Taylor Young Morton, David and Kathryn Allen, Teresa Edmondson, Sally McGhee, John Wittry, Jerry Jerome, Wendy Alfus-Rothman, Tom Boyer, Andrew Muntz, Paul Kay, Vincent Dupont, Mark Lurie, AJ Berkeley, Jose Marcelo Tam Malaga (Pepe), Dan Hogan, Louis Carter, Patrick Carmichael, Jon Peters, Prajna Horn, Sondra Ford, Richard Noble, Claudia Thair, Charlie and Pam Hedges, Laszlo Retfalvi, Lois Valerga, Lynn Timerman, John Leland, Sherry Bender, Merv Donner, Susan Cullen, Jack Cullen, Len Dinnocenzo, John Hamerski, Tracie Charland, Glenn and Suzanne Hayes, Linda Watkins, Manijeh Motaghy, Willem van Esch, Wendy Newman, Carolyn Bivens, and Vivette Payne.

There are also several clients that I would like to thank for their vision, courage, and dedication to accountability and B State breakthrough change to create new business paradigms, including Dr. Edward Ellison, Julie Miller-Phipps, Paul Riley, Stephanie Jo Gomez, Frank Dulcich, George Potter, Susan Achmatowicz, Sally MacKinnon, Mathias van Alphen, Marc Fields, Vic Koelsch, Jacques Roos, Pascal Zammit, Yves Barthelet, Alison Moore, Madhu Balachandran, Susan Juris, Vanessa Sowell, Fadi Diya, Craig Robbins, Greg Nichols, Jennifer Love, John Glanzer, Dave Gravender, Damian Goldvarg, Steve Sharon, Annette Shaked, Jamie McCamus, Elaine Vincent, Jim Barnes, John Jeter, Diane Davenport, Stephen Kapinus, Anne Novak, Mark Macellaro, Mark McNeil, Bruno Van Wonterghem, Bert Hensley, Al Cornish, Thomas Vehec, Eric Larson, Reid Tracy, Margaret Latif, Sally McGhee, Edward Fitzgerald Jr., Anthony Mire-Sluis, Steven Kowalski, Meribeth Germino, William O'Connell, Ira Needleman, Kathrene Hansen, (Friedkin), Gary O'Dell, James Tsai, Leon Ranzana, David Sanders, Patrick Carroll, Jamie Woolf, Kathy LaMarr-Bines, Fritz Smith, Scott Lockhart, Jonathan Lee, Jin Chon, Rich Abreu,

Kees van Langen, Elizabeth Schulz, Yar-Khan, Syed Abbas, Joe Marques, Christina Campbell, Tara and Dave Marino, Mike Noone, Gene Gerrard, John Parrott, Darlene Crowder, Audrey Chan, Kevin Osborne, Candy Spitzer, Wendy Fletcher, Zainab Salbi, Mary Zients, Gene Thin Elk, Robin Innes, Lois Lukens, Paul Trinidad, Lois Vallerga, Anthony Shaw, Michelle Rochwarger, Jamie McManus, Sandra Summers, Brenda Raine, Runa Bouius, Naila Moloo, Praful Kulkani, Reid Tracy, Margarete Nielsen, and Mary Ann Munro.

About the Author

MARK SAMUEL, founder and CEO of IMPAQ, has served as a thought leader for developing accountable leaders and creating accountable organizations for over thirty years. He is the author of *Creating the Accountable Organization* and the award-winning *Making Yourself Indispensable: The Power of Personal Accountability*, and he regularly speaks on the topic of business and culture transformation. Mark has been featured on CNBC and Bloomberg, as well as Fast Company, Forbes, and *Fortune* magazine, as a top authority on accountable leadership, teamwork, and culture. His work has extended across the globe with executives, senior leadership, and middle-management teams to achieve breakthrough results in industries including technology, health care, pharma-bio, utility, manufacturing, retail, higher education, government, and nonprofit. Mark earned his master's degree in business management from the University of California, Irvine, and a master's degree in spiritual psychology from the University of Santa Monica. He resides with his wife, Kamin, in San Clemente, California. Website: www.marksamuel.com.

Join us in growing the B State Community and benefit from rich resources and the opportunity to network with your peers on a similar journey. Visit www.BState.com/bonus to get access to videos, webinars, and other tools on how to draft and refine your B State to deliver breakthrough results.